*"We not only saved the world, er, saved the banks
and led the way."*

(Jeering)
*"The Opposition may not like the fact that we led the world
in saving the banking system, but we did."*

GORDON BROWN, Prime Minister, House of Commons,
Wednesday 10th December 2008,
during Prime Minister's Questions.

Published under licence 2012 by Searching Finance Ltd

ISBN: 978-1-907720-56-7

Cover photo: Lol Keegan

Typeset and designed by Deirdré Gyenes

"Saving the World?"

Gordon Brown reconsidered

By William Keegan

About the author

WILLIAM KEEGAN is the Senior Economics Commentator of the *Observer*, for which he has written a regular column for many years. He was educated at Wimbledon College and Trinity College, Cambridge. He worked briefly for the *Daily Mail City Page* in the 1960s, before joining the *Financial Times*, where he was Economics Correspondent for nine years. After a spell at the Bank of England, where he edited the economic commentary in the Bank's Quarterly Bulletin, he moved on to the *Observer*.

William Keegan is a frequent broadcaster. Among his many books are: Mrs Thatcher's Economic Experiment; Mr Lawson's Gamble; Britain Without Oil; The Spectre of Capitalism; 2066 and all that; Who Runs the Economy? (with Rupert Pennant-Rea); and The Prudence of Mr Gordon Brown.

About Searching Finance

Searching Finance publishes economics, finance and politics.
Check out our website:
www.searchingfinance.com

Follow us on Facebook:
http://www.facebook.com/searchingfinance

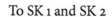

To SK 1 and SK 2

CONTENTS

ACKNOWLEDGEMENTS

I SHOULD LIKE TO THANK the many people in public life who have generously spared the time to help me with this monograph. Most conversations took place on " background" terms. But it was interesting that even those who had an axe to grind about the way they had been treated by Gordon Brown agreed that the reaction against him had gone too far. I was struck in particular by the remark by one senior official with whom Brown had had many an altercation :

> "Do you know, he was the only man in public life to telephone me to wish me luck before I had an operation, and the only man to ring afterwards to make sure I was all right."

I should also like to thank the publisher, Ashwin Rattan, who approached me with the idea, and James Jinks and Michelle Clement, of Queen Mary, University of London, who helped to track down some written sources, as well as giving technical advice when "work in progress" moved from my lovingly preserved Olympia manual typewriter to an ipad. My thanks are also due to the distinguished broadcaster Michael Cockerell for valuable help.

My thanks also go to those friends, and one relation, who read the manuscript and offered invaluable comments, namely: Steve Richards, Adam Raphael, Adrian Hamilton, Jon Davis, John Steadman and Victor Keegan. As usual, however, the buck stops with the author.

PREFACE

BEFORE TAKING over the prime ministerial reins from Tony Blair in June 2007, Gordon Brown had been the longest serving Chancellor of the Exchequer since Nicholas Vansittart, who was in that office from 1812 to 1823.

Brown, with Blair himself and Peter Mandelson, was one of the principal architects of New Labour, the 'reformed' and 'modernised' political creature that emerged from the ashes of the wounding defeats of 1983 and 1992. If Brown had remained at No. 11 Downing Street a mere six months longer, he would have beaten Vansittart's length of tenure, and been outdistanced only by the formidable 18th century politician Robert Walpole, who was Chancellor from 1715 to 1717, and again, for a truly remarkable stretch from 1721 to 1742.

Unlike Brown, Walpole was also prime minister during both those periods. Gordon Brown would have loved to combine both jobs. Indeed, there were times when some observers thought he was such a powerful and obtrusive Chancellor that, in practice, he did. As that canny student of power politics Anthony Sampson observed in his last book, "Brown had acquired almost unprecedented scope as Chancellor." Again, the commentator Anatole Kaletsky observed of the 2005 pre-election Budget: "Before Brown, budget speeches used to be about running the economy. Now they are about running the whole country."

Not only was Brown Chancellor for a long time: he was also feted as an extraordinarily successful one. He began by making a virtue, not always associated with the Labour Party, of fiscal prudence. He was acclaimed for making the Bank of England independent, and for presiding over a long period of low inflation and steady economic growth. For a time people who should have known better even wanted to believe that he had succeeded in his rash promise to abolish 'boom and bust.' True, within the Labour Party there were 'Old Labour' colleagues who would curse him for not being 'Labour' enough. But in the real world of an electorate, a largely Conservative press and financial markets of which New Labour always seemed nervous, he felt that he had to make compromises. Such compromises - for example, accepting the 40 per cent top rate of tax introduced in 1988 by Nigel Lawson- undoubtedly helped him to gain the temporary allegiance of a wider audience than natural Labour voters. His strategy was to proceed by stealth when it came to assisting the people he genuinely cared about most, namely the poor and the otherwise disadvantaged.

Yet, after this celebrated Chancellor achieved his ultimate ambition of becoming prime minister, it all seemed to end in tears. As far as his own country is concerned, he appears to have gone "from hero to zero". This is partly because his premiership, the job for which he had fought ruthlessly for all those years, is deemed to been a disaster; but also because, with the onset of the financial crisis of 2007 onwards, his chancellorship has also been seen in a new, deeply unfavourable light. The good things, such as the impressive effort by both Blair and Brown, to improve education, health and other public services, have largely been taken for granted. And the foolhardy commitment to abolish boom and bust has been seen for what it always was.

Not least, there has been the question of Brown's character and behaviour. Here the heart of the problem seems to have been Brown's reluctance to stand against Blair for the leadership way back in 1994, after the untimely death of Labour's "Lost Leader" John Smith. A running sore developed into a chronic wound, which affected Brown's behaviour not only towards Blair, but towards many around him. Brown felt that, in accordance with the so called Granita Agreement (apparently made shortly before the famous dinner at a now defunct Islington restaurant) Blair should have stepped down a lot earlier than he did. Eventually he wore Blair down, and managed to contrive a kind of coronation, without an internal party election, in June 2007.

The conventional wisdom is that, after a promising few months, Brown's premiership fell apart, and that his big mistake lay in not calling a general election in October 2007. The realisation of his ambition appeared to consume him.

It is the purpose of this monograph to try to redress the balance. In my view, for all the domestic problems, Brown was the right leader, in the right place, at the right time to give an impressive display of world leadership in the face of the economic crisis. The world is by no means through this crisis, but Brown's initiative, experience and sheer determination and will power played a major role in warding off the threat of a world economic catastrophe in 2008-2009. And, among other things, Brown must surely be credited with sound judgement in keeping the UK out of the euro when he was being heavily pressurised by his prime minister and most of the Establishment.

The man whom his mentor John Smith once described as "the most intelligent man I know" deserves, to my mind, more credit than he has so far received.

Notes, references and further reading:

Servants of the People: The Inside Story of New Labour, Andrew Rawnsley 2000
The End of the Party: The Rise and Fall of New Labour, Andrew Rawnsley 2010

INTRODUCTION

IN MY BOOK 'The Prudence of Mr Gordon Brown' I examined the early life of Gordon Brown and the influences on him; his political career up to the time of his arrival at the Treasury in 1997; his chancellorship during New Labour's first term from 1997 to 2001; and the greater part of the second, 2001-05 term.

The second, paperback edition of the book broke off in the summer of 2004, by which time Brown had equalled Lloyd George's record of seven consecutive years at the Treasury. Indeed, Brown had become the longest serving chancellor since Nicholas Vansittart (1812-23). What is more, he was widely fêted, both at home and abroad, even praised by many of his natural opponents in the Conservative press. He went on to serve a further three years as chancellor, making ten years all told.

Few of Brown's speeches at the time were complete without boastful references to the long period of economic growth over which he had presided. Indeed, just over a year later Mervyn King, whom he had made governor of the Bank of England in succession to Eddie George, was to be heard proclaiming that the economy had experienced 53 successive quarters of growth which he had described as "wholly unprecedented".

At the time it was difficult to fault Brown. As someone who had known and admired him since the mid-1980s, I myself was broadly sympathetic to what he was trying to achieve, but in 'Prudence' I expressed some unfashionable doubts about his

1

strategy. Thus, although his Conservative predecessor Kenneth Clarke had proved a popular chancellor, presiding over a good economic recovery from the travails of the pound's ill-fated membership of the European exchange rate mechanism, and restoring the budgetary position, there had been many years of neglect of health, education and the nation's infrastructure. Moreover, for all John Major's genuine feelings for the poor, and the background from which he hailed, there had been a marked increase in inequality under the Conservatives in general, and not just under Margaret Thatcher.

Yet when Brown assumed office, he made such a virtue of his proclaimed 'prudence' and fiscal rules that he continued a two-year freeze on public expenditure that had been instituted by Clarke but to which Clarke himself later admitted he had no intention of adhering. The result was that New Labour in its first 1997-2001 term spent less on investment in infrastructure than the previous Thatcher/Major administrations had in comparable four-year periods.

Brown was also so haunted by the long period in which Labour had been out of office – since 1979! – that he was as cautious, not to say pusillanimous, as his colleagues Tony Blair and Peter Mandelson when it came to doing something to alleviate poverty. True, he devoted much of his time at the Treasury to what economists call 'redistribution' – all those complex 'tax credits' – but it was done in a clandestine fashion. As with his approach to taxation, the operative phrase was 'proceeding by stealth.'

Desperate to be elected, and with unhappy memories of the way his mentor John Smith had been pilloried for daring to threaten tax increases in his 'shadow budget' preceding the 1992 general election, Brown went along with Blair in committing the Party to a self-denying ordinance: not to raise the basic or the higher rates of income tax during that first term – a commitment which was renewed. And there was of course Peter Mandelson's notorious remark that he had no problem

2

with people being "filthy rich". Such a remark would never have been made by Brown, but it reinforced the worst suspicions harboured about New Labour by the old 'Left.'

The 'prudence' for which Brown was so admired by many commentators, not least on the right and in the financial markets, was always 'for a purpose.' Once the first Labour chancellor since Denis Healey (chancellor 1974-79) had established his credentials, he could then be more ambitiously 'Labour'. But there was another purpose: the purpose of eventually becoming prime minister, a goal he had apparently been aiming at since childhood, and towards which he devoted so much of his energy while at No. 11.

The destructive nature of Brown's continual manoeuvring to unseat Blair has been examined exhaustively in many places, not least in my Observer colleague Andrew Rawnsley's work. It seemed to many observers – those close to him, as well as most outsiders – that, having schemed so long for the top job, Brown did not know what to do when he got there. Certainly, even if he did know, his obsessive personality, inability to delegate and intrinsic disorganisation were to prove inimical to a harmonious and successful premiership. It had been said by the Tory grandee Lord Salisbury that the politician Iain Macleod was "too clever by half." Brown had been credited with all the manner of strategic insights; yet when it came to the chance to win 'a mandate' after taking over from Tony Blair, he funked it. Thus, after a few glorious months in the summer of 2007 when he won respect, he allowed speculation about an autumn election to get out of hand, and then changed his mind. Indecisiveness is not a quality associated with great leaders.

After that, it was, in the conventional view, all downhill. In my earlier book I referred to "the 'imprudence' that, ironically, may lie behind the prudence." I had witnessed 'feast and famine' or 'famine and feast' before in British economic policy – not least under the Heath premiership of 1970-74, when a proto-Thatcherite approach to squeezing the economy gave way, after a 'U' turn, to a boom in public spending and credit creation which ended in tears.

In 'The Prudence of Mr Gordon Brown' I worried that, although the independent Bank of England and Monetary Policy Committee were widely considered to be huge successes, 'imbalances' were becoming apparent in the economy, with the exchange rate too high, manufacturing suffering and too much reliance being placed on 'services'. There was "an old fashioned consumer boom... encouraged by low interest rates and rising house prices."

Gordon Brown believed in the latter phase of his chancellorship that his earlier prudence had been worth it, because a Labour chancellor was now able to borrow vast sums for public sector investment without the financial markets batting an eyelid. And then...

Thus I think I can make a reasonable claim to have been more sceptical about certain aspects of Gordon Brown's chancellorial achievements than many of what proved to be his fair weather supporters.

On the other hand, I now find that, if anything, the reaction against Gordon Brown, both as chancellor and prime minister, has been overdone. It is the purpose of the following chapters to provide what I hope will be considered a reasonably balanced view.

Notes, references and further reading:

See:

The Prudence of Mr Gordon Brown, William Keegan, 2003 and 2004

Moving Britain Forward, Selected Speeches 1997-2006, Gordon Brown

CHAPTER 1

FROM HERO TO ZERO

MUCH VILIFIED in later years, Gordon Brown was sufficiently popular in the country at large for Tony Blair to recall him to the heart of the 2005 election campaign, after initially isolating him. Blair's electoral handicap was simple: he had committed British forces to the invasion of Iraq on a false prospectus. Whatever Brown's role in the run-up to the invasion of 2003, and however difficult he was in private, both with Blair and, it now appears, many others, he was a popular chancellor. The granting of independence to the Bank of England by a Labour chancellor – independence to determine monetary policy: the size, direction and timing of changes in interest rates – was widely seen as a huge success. The removal of the management of the gilt (government debt) market from the Bank of England to a separate office had upset the then governor Eddie George, but was of little interest to the general public. And, until the onset of the financial crisis in 2007-09, when the deficiencies of the regulatory structure were laid bare, the removal of bank regulation from Threadneedle Street had also had little impact on the wider world.

Observers like myself might complain that an overvalued exchange rate was distorting the pattern of growth, and not in the long-term interest of British industry or the economy (all those 'imbalances'); but Eddie George (governor from 1993 to 2003) would say that "unbalanced growth is better than no growth" and his successor Mervyn King christened it 'the NICE decade' – an acronym for 'non-inflationary consistently expansionary'.

Yet problems were building up, even before the 2007 crisis. Thus manufacturing output fell in four of the six years from 2001 to 2006, and was no higher in 2006 that it had been in 2000. Meanwhile services, not least financial services (the City) were roaring away, expanding by almost 30 per cent over the same period (2000 to 2006).

The 1980s, principally under the chancellorship of Nigel Lawson (1983-89) had been the first decade in living memory when the growth of consumers' expenditure had outpaced that of real incomes, the gap being filled by borrowing – that is, credit expansion. Official credit controls had largely been abolished in the early to mid-1980s, and Nigel Lawson – like Brown after him, widely praised for much of the chancellorship – had been the object of intense criticism towards the end of his tenure at No. 11 for the way the consumer boom was generally perceived to have got out of control.

Indeed, the slogan that was to haunt Brown to this day – the claim that he had abolished 'boom and bust' – derived from the time when Brown had been attacking chancellor Lawson with some aplomb from the opposition benches. The original claim was that there would be "no more Tory boom and bust". The pedantic excuse for Brown is that he did emphasise TORY boom and bust, but the excuse was never going to wash. For a chancellor who was also an historian, it was a rash claim. He won kudos at the time for his successful assault on Lawson, but promising that 'busts' were things of the past was to prove of short-term political benefit, and a hostage to fortune.

Yet there are those officials in the Treasury who maintain that estimates and criticism of the so-called 'Brown Boom' have been overdone. The rate of growth of household consumer expenditure slowed down during New Labour's second term – the sequence being 4.5 per cent real growth in 2002, 3.3 per cent in 2003, 3.1 per cent in 2004, 2.2 per cent in 2005 and 1.8 per cent in 2006, with a brief jump to 2.7 per cent in 2007. The problem was that the growth of real incomes, reflecting the cumulative effects of the impact of globalisation and competition from China on the incomes of the more advanced industrial countries, slowed markedly. Thus real household disposable incomes rose by over 16 per cent in total during the four years from 2000 to 2003 inclusive, but by a mere 6 per cent during the following four years, 2004-2007 inclusive.

The slowing pace was accompanied by a significant decline in consumer confidence, with the Treasury's favourite index for this falling in every one of those last four years. There was rapid growth in consumer credit until 2005, at which point, the growth rate halved to around 7 per cent by 2006-07.

Ironically, if there was a Brown Boom, it was a lot less spectacular than the Lawson Boom. During the last six years of his chancellorship consumer expenditure by households rose by less than 20 per cent, whereas during Lawson's six-year chancellorship it shot up by almost 33 per cent. There were few officials in Brown's Treasury whose experience or memories went back to the Lawson years; but the few survivors claim that the Brown Boom had been much exaggerated by critics with axes to grind.

And there were to be plenty of those, not least on the government benches when the Conservatives returned to power in 2010. It was true that (well before the financial crisis of 2007-08) even the most patient of independent think tanks, such as the National Institute of Economic and Social Research, had been concluding that there was a smell of 'fudge' in the air. Brown was hoist by his own petard in that he had boasted so much about the fiscal rules which had earned him that early reputation for prudence, but had later redefined the measurement of the so-called 'economic cycle' in order to justify higher borrowing. Nevertheless, for all the fuss generated by the incoming government about the deficit and the inheritance, net public sector debt as a percentage of gross domestic product (GDP) was higher, during the last two financial years of the Major government (1995-96; 1996-97) than in any year under New Labour until the full force of the financial crisis hit home in 2008-09. The ratio was 41.9 per cent and 42.5 per cent in the last Major years. It fell to 40.6 per cent in 1997-98 and to as low as 29.7 per cent in 2001-02, reflecting the determined way that Brown went about demonstrating his fiscal rectitude during that first 1997-2001 term.

After that, with the initial two-year freeze well and truly over, and Brown feeling that he had established New Labour's reputation for fiscal rectitude, and had won the scope to fulfil his heart-felt ambition to do something about poverty, the brakes were well and truly eased. Believer though he was in a better health service, the chancellor was not amused by his prime minister's promise on television one Sunday morning to bring the level of health expenditure up to Continental standards within a relatively short time, because this commitment had obvious implications for expenditure elsewhere, and control of overall public spending is the Treasury's fiefdom.

There is little doubt that the chancellor played hard and fast with his fiscal rules: even the most liberal Keynesians believe that the aim should be to balance the current budget in the medium to long run, which means that it is storing up trouble for the future to run a deficit in times of plenty. But as the debate raging under the Cameron/Osborne administration shows, we Keynesians still have a hard time trying to woo people away from 'household economics' and to establish the point that deficits are essential if the economy is to stand a chance of emerging from recession or depression. What matters, in the end, is the balance of the economy, not the budget.

However, even though Brown's stewardship was wanting when it came to balancing the budget during the good days, the fact of the matter, almost universally ignored by his critics, is that until the advent of the financial crisis, the ratio of net debt to GDP was by no means alarming. Indeed, at 35.9 per cent in 2006-07 it was still well below the outcome in any of the years of the Kenneth Clarke chancellorship of 1993-97.

The killer blow was the financial crisis, which took its toll both on revenue and expenditure, including the cost of bailing out the banks. When the Conservatives go on about 'the deficit' and 'the inheritance' they are actually talking about developments after Brown's chancellorship. Thus the net debt to GDP ratio rose sharply to 43.3 per cent in 2008-09, 52.8 per cent in 2009-10 and 59.9 per cent in 2010-11.

Notes, references and further reading:

1) Re Iraq and "false prospectus". See Robin Cook's Resignation Speech, 17 March 2003, reprinted in: Robin Cook, The Point of Departure, 2003.

2) Statistics quoted in this chapter come from the Office for National Statistics and HM Treasury.

3) A welcome corrective to the near hysteria generated by the incoming Conservative/ Liberal/ Democrat Coalition from 2007 onwards is contained in The National Debt in Perspective, by Professor Robert Neild, a former chief economic adviser to HM Treasury. (Royal Economic Society Newsletter, January 2012).

CHAPTER 2
A CRISIS NOT ENTIRELY OF BROWN'S MAKING

WE COME TO Brown's premiership, 27 June 2007 to 11 May 2010, and Alistair Darling's chancellorship. Brown's favourite joke for public occasions in his early days at the Treasury was: "There are two kinds of chancellor: those who fail and those who get out in time." In the early years he was perceived to have had many successes – fiscal rectitude, the independence of the Bank of England, continuous non-inflationary growth etc. – and summer 2007 seemed, on the face of it, a 'just in time' moment to move on.

Not that he had wanted to wait that long. On the contrary, he had been manoeuvring for the succession to Tony Blair for many years; indeed, if he had had his way, he would not have been at the Treasury long enough to beat Lloyd George's record of seven consecutive years, let alone be there longer than any chancellor since the first quarter of the 19th century.

When Gordon Brown moved next door to No. 10 he had been chancellor for ten years. Less well known to the domestic electorate, he had also been chairman of the International Monetary Fund's key policymaking committee, the IMFC. In this capacity he had made vitally important contacts in the rest of the G7 (US, Japan, Germany, France, Italy and Canada) which were going to stand him in good stead when the world economy appeared to be on the edge of a precipice in 2008-09 – when, in his own Freudian slip, he "saved the world."

In one sense, Brown got out in time. In another, he most certainly did not. By moving next door, and by trying to maintain a grip on economic policy, to the chagrin of his successor as chancellor, Alistair Darling, Brown stayed right there in the centre, a prospective sacrificial victim to the many in the Conservative Party and elsewhere who were looking for a scapegoat. He was still there; they did not have to look far.

The first thing that should be said – and it should not need saying, but the force of the anti-Brown propaganda has been formidable – is that Gordon Brown was not responsible for the world economic crisis. True, he was very much a participant in the world of policymakers and advisers who accepted the conventional wisdom that globalisation was a good thing, that independent central banks and inflation-targeting were the latest version of the economic philosopher's stone, and that the sophistication of the financial system was such that risk had been spread almost to the point of elimination. This latter point naturally provokes hollow laughter these days, yet I was a member of the audience at a meeting of the Society of Business Economists at the Bank of England in September 2002 when the then chairman of the US Federal Reserve, Alan Greenspan, had put this preposterous proposition to the audience with a straight, if lugubrious (Greenspan often looked lugubrious) face. There were sceptical questions at the time, but there was not much hollow laughter.

And when the economist Raghuram G. Rajan questioned the conventional wisdom at a symposium on the 'Greenspan Doctrine' in 2005, he was subjected to brutal criticism by leading colleagues and disciples of Greenspan's.

The occasion was the annual gathering of great and good central bankers, monetary officials and economists organised by the Federal Reserve of Kansas, at Jackson Hole in Wyoming.

Rajan's prescient and perceptive warning of the perils of rapid credit creation, asset price inflation and the complexity of the financial system were airily dismissed by, among others, Don Kohn, subsequently deputy chairman of the Federal Reserve, and Lawrence Summers, then President of Harvard, formerly US Treasury Secretary under President Clinton and a most distinguished economist.

The onset of the crisis in 2007-08 introduced the general public to the world of obscure 'financial products' whose functions remained mysterious but the impact of whose malfunctioning was there for all to see. It was this financial jungle, 'mortgage-backed securities' (MBSs), 'securitised loans', 'credit default swaps' and 'collateralised debt obligations' (CDOs) that had allegedly reduced and diversified financial risk. In Kohn's paean of praise for the Greenspan doctrine, these financial 'products' had "made institutions more robust" and "by facilitating the flow of savings across markets and national boundaries, these developments have contributed to a better allocation of resources and promoted growth." By contrast, the kind of regulation after the Great Crash of 1929 and the 1929-32 Great Depression were now contemptuously dismissed. For Kohn "the actions of private individuals to protect themselves – what chairman Greenspan has called private regulation – are generally quite effective." The hubris did not end there: by contrast, government "risks undermining private regulation and financial stability by undermining incentives."

This cavalier dismissal was in response to Rajan's observation that some of these incentives were actually "perverse", encouraging investment managers and financial operators generally to take on more risks, because their bonuses were geared to the apparent financial returns taking such risks generated. I say 'apparent', because the subsequent crisis demonstrated just how bogus many of these 'investment returns' actually were. Rajan warned that "the linkages between markets, and between markets and institutions, are now more pronounced...it exposes the system to large systemic shocks – large shifts in asset prices or changes in aggregate liquidity."

Rajan himself is also a distinguished economist, and at the time also happened to be chief economist at the IMF. But he had dared to challenge the Greenspan Doctrine. At the time Greenspan's reputation could hardly have been higher. He was referred to only half-jokingly as Master of the Universe, and widely considered to have steered the US economy, and therefore the rest of the world, through some stormy seas, and to have been as successful as could be hoped by achieving the Fed's twin constitutional goals of price stability and high employment (unlike the European Central Bank, whose brief is price stability).

For Greenspan and his many disciples all was (almost) for the best in the world as they knew it. Gordon Brown was a follower of Greenspan's. He had consulted him over whether to make the Bank of England independent; had invited him to open the newly furbished Treasury building opposite St James's Park; and even arranged for him to visit his home town of Kirkcaldy in Scotland, for a kind of pilgrimage to honour Adam Smith. It did not take much detective work to conclude who was behind the award of an honorary knighthood to Greenspan in 2002. Indeed, there were those in Westminster and Whitehall who regarded Brown's near worship of Greenspan as reminiscent of the bobbysoxers of the 1950s – excitable fans of film stars and pop stars.

Responsibility for the financial crisis, like the mysterious workings of the market in 'financial engineering', was spread far and wide. There was a consensus; in JK Galbraith's phrase, it was the 'conventional wisdom' that the central banks, by apparently controlling consumer price inflation, were successfully steering their respective economies, while the financial system was superb at spreading risk.

True, some economists were concerned about the inflation of asset prices, and about the rapid growth of credit. But it was no longer fashionable to devote much attention to the credit statistics. And insofar as there was a debate about asset prices, the worried economists never got very far in the debate, and there were always objections about how difficult it would be.

One of the most prominent objectors to the conventional wisdom was William White, then chief economist at the Bank for International Settlements in Basle. His warnings were stronger in his speeches than they were in the prestigious BIS annual reports, where the central banking consensus managed to water them down. Even so, the message of trouble in store was unmistakable for several years before the calamities of 2007/2008.

Brown can be blamed for being a prominent member of the consensus; but he was accompanied by the Treasury itself, and the Bank of England. "To be frank," one Whitehall official conceded in a private conversation, which he was happy to be reflected in print but not attributed, "we messed up. The Treasury messed up. The Bank messed up. The Financial Services Authority messed up. The Treasury has not served Labour chancellors well."

Brown and his team were ultimately responsible for the removal of banking supervision from the Bank of England, and the tripartite division of responsibility for what has now become known as 'macro-prudential financial regulation' between the Treasury, the Bank and the FSA. It was, alas, as things turned out, a case of 'divide and rule' – or, rather, divide and not rule, but actually try to make a virtue out of 'light touch regulation.'

Ironically, one of the motives behind the removal of supervision from the Bank was that the Bank had got egg on its face twice during the 1980s, over failures of supervision in the case of Johnson Matthey Bankers and Bank of Credit and Commerce International (BCCI). The Bank had still been left with the responsibility for financial stability in the Brownian reforms of 1997 onwards, but, by common consent, in Mervyn

15

King it had a governor whose main interest lay in everything to do with achieving the inflation target – or explaining, in latter years, why it had not been achieved. Nevertheless, when it erupted the crisis was not confined to the poorly regulated City of London. It was much broader than that.

Notes, references and further reading:

1) A good account of the atmosphere of the times, and the way Rajan's warnings were dismissed, is contained in *How Markets Fail*, John Cassidy, 2009.

2) The crisis introduced the layperson to the world of "derivatives". It is a complex world, based on the simple definition that, "a derivative instrument is a contract whose value depends on, or derives from, the value of an underlying asset or index". Gluttons for punishment could put a cold towel over their heads and consult the authoritative: Derivatives in Plain Words, Hong Kong Monetary Authority, 1997.

CHAPTER 3

BUST AFTER BOOM –

A 'SOUNDBITE' BITES BACK

EVEN THOUGH Gordon Brown is far from being the sole culprit to be blamed for the financial crisis, the words that will haunt him forever are 'boom and bust'. It matters not that reports of the Brown Boom have been much exaggerated. It matters not that the expansion of consumer spending and borrowing in the Brown years was appreciably less than during Lawson's 1983-89 chancellorship. What matters is that there was a 'bust' that permeated the G7 advanced industrial countries – a notable exception being the strength of the Canadian banking system. It was a 'bust' that brought us the biggest peacetime financial and economic crisis since the Great Depression of 1929-32, and it demonstrated to the world that the classic 'boom and bust' cycle associated with finance capitalism since the 18th century had not been abolished.

"Gordon," said a senior Continental official who had had many dealings with Brown over the years, "had his flaws. But I greatly respect him, and have always been impressed by the way he does not just speak from a brief, but intelligently pursues the discussion, constantly taking notes." This gentleman paused, and added: "What a mistake it was to claim that you abolished the cycle."

The adverse criticisms of Brown and his immediate circle are legion. But one that shocked my informant most, and indeed shook me, was the reported response of a Brown aide when the point was made in private discussions that housing had been a seriously neglected area under New Labour. By comparison with the great days in the early to mid-1950s when Harold Macmillan, as Minister for Housing, could boast of actually having achieved his ambitious target of building 300,000 new dwellings a year, New Labour's record was abysmal. True, Macmillan had notoriously cut corners and relaxed standards (not safety standards); and true the Thatcher/Major governments were also negligent. But neglect during the Thatcher years was all the more reason for New Labour to attempt to redress the situation.

The extent of the neglect of housing in the UK during recent decades has been lucidly analysed by Dr Eoin Clarke, in 'Private Renters – the Forgotten Millions who Abandoned Labour' (The Red Book, Searching Finance). Under the Thatcher 'Right to Buy' scheme the Conservatives sold 2 million council homes but replaced only a quarter (585,000 out of 2 million). "This means that from 1980 housing waiting lists have grown. Today 5 million men, women and children are on housing waiting lists for social homes, 45,000 are homeless and 4 million families struggle with £8,500 private rent bills as a result of the Tories' actions."

Under the Blair governments "the number of council sales… dramatically increased and the building of social housing halted. The UK's population grew 4.41 million under Labour but the number of social homes continued to fall. A socialist (sic) PM did not see fit to invest in social housing."

Dr Clarke is not opposed to the concept of council house sales. "The Right to Buy (RTB) scheme launched by Margaret Thatcher in 1981 was initially a good thing. It enabled people with no stake in society, who had been paying rent faithfully all their lives, finally to get on the property ladder and build an inheritance for their children."

The problem was that councils were forbidden to retain the proceeds of sales of public sector housing; house building no longer remained a priority; and the rate of new building fell sharply. This had the effect of driving the poor homeless into the private rented sector, with all the familiar problems associated with unscrupulous landlords and the rising cost to the taxpayer of subsidising rents.

The obvious solution was a Macmillan-style building programme for social housing. One should have thought that this might appeal to Gordon Brown, who most certainly felt strongly about poverty. But, by contrast with Macmillan's ambitious targets all those years ago, under the Brown premiership the rate of new building for social housing was a somewhat inadequate 400 dwellings a year.

Here one comes up against the context in which the social goals of the Brown entourage appear to have clashed with the desire to continue riding on the crest of a wave of well-being associated with the asset price boom.

Thus, at one meeting under Brown as prime minister to discuss the general scene, one aide suggested that there was a serious housing crisis and an urgent need to build more social housing. To which someone who at the time was a trusted, if controversial, aide riposted: "If we did that it would hit house prices and we should lose the election."

A casual remark made like that on the spur of the moment is not exactly a basis for policy, but one fears it is all too indicative of the mood of the times. There were Cabinet colleagues of Brown's who felt strongly about the housing situation, and one actually said to me in desperation: "Can't YOU write something about it?"

The boom in asset prices in general and house prices in particular has by now become notorious for its 'distributional effects' – the way the 'haves' and 'possessors' did well out of the house price boom, but many natural Labour voters in rented accommodation did not. There has also been much discussion since about the 'inter-generational' effects, the argument being that the so-called 'baby-boomers did well' but that getting on the housing ladder is much tougher for their children. In practice the position is more complicated, because a great deal of 'inter-generational' compensation takes place within families. Nevertheless, the conventional view that rising house prices were a 'good thing' – see press headlines *passim* during both the period of the Lawson Boom and Brown Boom – did not fit too well with the neglect of social housing.

Apart from anything else, the neglect of housing has manifestly aggravated discontent about immigration. Between them, the main British political parties have removed many of the traditional ladders that enabled people from working or lower middle class backgrounds to 'better themselves'. The route for many families in the 1950s and 1960s was to move from private rented accommodation to a rented council house and then, eventually, to a house or flat of their own. I know many people who benefited from this progression. My own family was one.

This is not to say that Gordon Brown had no feelings for the homeless or the poor in general when it came to housing. But the bulk of his efforts in this direction seemed to be aimed at 'housing benefit' to assist those who were too poor to pay a market rent, rather than towards a serious housing drive. In this, it must be said, Brown was far from the only politician to fail to act to address the seriousness of the situation.

As for the belief of one of Brown's advisers that rising house prices were a useful, if undeclared, element in the electoral platform, I am reminded of the time my friend, the late Lord Alexander, after being made chairman of NatWest, visited the Bundesbank during the Lawson Boom. He was carrying a copy of the business section of one of the broadsheets, which contained a headline proclaiming something to the effect of

'Good news: house prices rise again'. On glancing at it, the then president of the Bundesbank, Karl-Otto Pohl, said: "In this country, that would be bad news."

Notes, references and further reading:

1) The financial crisis of 2007 onwards hit economic activity and employment badly. But if there was one area where production was boosted it was in books about the crisis. Among these are: *The Gods that Failed*, Larry Elliott and Dan Atkinson, 2008; *The Financial Crisis*, Howard Davies, 2010; *The Trouble With Markets*, Roger Bootle, 2011; *Fault Lines*, Raghuram G. Rajan, 2010; *Skidelsky on The Economic Crisis 2008-2011*, Centre for Global Studies, 2012, and *The Crunch*, Alex Brummer, 2008.

The late Andrew Glyn's Capitalism Unleashed was published in 2006, but provides a very readable account of the international background, as does Globalisation by M. Panic, 2011. And for a deep historical perspective there is the widely quoted and ironically entitled *This Time Is Different*, Carmen M. Reinhart & Kenneth S. Rogoff.

2) The senior Continental official and others: I have drawn on many background conversations with politicians, civil servants and bankers. The practice has grown up in recent years for authors to put footnotes in the text, only for the reader to find endless references to "private information". In this monograph I intend to spare the reader this fruitless search. Trust me!

3) Re housing and other areas of domestic policy under New Labour. *The Verdict*, by Polly Toynbee and David Walker gives a comprehensive and fair account. Housing policy may have left a lot to be desired, "Yet under Labour child poverty showed its sharpest fall for decades, and the UK showed the biggest drop in the EU." This point is echoed by former Labour "rebel" M.P. Bob Marshall-Andrews in Off Message, 2011. No friend of Gordon Brown's, the author gives him full credit for the reduction in poverty he observes over the years in his constituency.

CHAPTER 4
'NICE' WHILE IT LASTED

To PROMISE to abolish boom and bust was foolhardy and it is doubtful whether the promise had much to do with Labour's electoral victory in 1997. What is more convincing is the view that re-election in both 2001 and 2005 was associated, if not with the belief that 'boom and bust' had been abolished, then with the general impression that, thanks largely to Gordon Brown, Labour had proved itself to be trustworthy in handling the nation's finances. What was more, as noted, it had presided over most of the years of what Mervyn King had christened a 'non-inflationary consistently expansionary' decade – the so called NICE decade – which had begun under the chancellorship of Kenneth Clarke, in the years of recovery from the travails of Black Wednesday on 16 September 1992.

Much of the credit for New Labour's three successive electoral victories – 1997, 2001 and 2005 – went to Tony Blair, and Blair continues to be praised, notwithstanding the deception over weapons of mass destruction and the fiasco of Iraq, for those three victories.

Yet history has been revised in many of these assessments, because, while people remember all too easily Gordon Brown's gaffe in the 2010 election campaign over 'that woman' in Rochdale, many seem to have forgotten that the 2005 campaign was going so badly for New Labour that, having been relegated by Blair to the sidelines of that campaign because of the tensions between them, Brown had to be called back in 2005 to rescue the situation.

For in 2005, while Blair was becoming increasingly unpopular because of Iraq, Brown was still something of a national hero. The granting of independence to the Bank of England was still widely hailed as an enormous success, with inflation well under control. Indeed, for some critics, inflation was almost under too much control, with the Consumer Price Index (CPI) rising at less than the official target of first 2.5 per cent, and later 2 per cent.

By 2005 the unemployment rate in the UK had come down from an average of 8.1 per cent in 1996 – the year before New Labour came to power – to an average of 4.8 per cent in 2004 and 4.9 per cent in 2005, or just under 1.5 million, against 2.3 million in 1996. Long-term unemployment – those out of work for over 12 months – had halved, and the figure for those out of work for over two years had fallen by almost four-fifths while New Labour was in office.

The general sense of well-being was borne out by the growth of retail sales and overall consumer spending. While not as dramatic as in the 1980s Lawson Boom (as noted earlier) the annual increase in spending during those years contrasted sharply with the post-2007 years. Thus the series of annual increases in retail sales from 2000 to 2004 inclusive was: 4.9 per cent; 6.0 per cent; 2.9 per cent; and 5.6 per cent. By contrast, in the four years from 2007 to 2011, the annual average increase was about 0.5 per cent – almost negligible. The impact of the recession was much greater on total consumer spending, which includes car purchases and services: spending fell by almost 5 per cent during that four-year period, 2008-11.

The 2005 election year had been preceded by a huge boom in house prices – the Nationwide index showed average prices rising by 10.6 per cent in 2001, 19.7 per cent in 2002, 19.4 per cent in 2003 and 17.1 per cent in 2004. Gordon Brown's reputation was high during these years, but it was to be a case of 'the higher they rise, the harder they fall.'

Notes, references and further reading:

1) Re Sir Mervyn King and the so-called "Nice" decade. The Governor was quick to emphasise that things would not continue like that. All his speeches are there on the Bank of England website, and it was widely noted that towards the latter phase of his second term Sir Mervyn became an almost notorious prophet of gloom and an outspoken critic of bankers.

2) The Office for National Statistics figures quoted here for retail sales are in volume terms, i.e. after adjusting for price increases.

CHAPTER 5
'I KNOW I HAVE TO TAKE THE RAP'

THROUGHOUT my career there has been a continual wailing chorus from businessmen and right wing politicians complaining about red tape, regulation and government intervention.

To a certain extent the ordinary citizen going about his or her daily life, or trying to, can sympathise with such complaints. "There are too many meddling, petty bureaucrats. Why don't they let us get on with our lives?" is a cry which most of us understand. There is a natural tendency for government officials, at national and local level, to interfere, and the results can often be very irritating. One has only to think of the excessive zeal with which certain councils operate their parking, or no-parking, regimes.

One also has sympathy with critics who point to the seemingly endless stream of new legislation that each new government brings. There is an inherent democratic problem here: governments are legislatures, and politicians are what the Americans refer to as 'lawmakers'. Introducing new laws and regulations is what government do, even when, paradoxically, the purpose of the new laws may be 'to deregulate'.

In the case of Gordon Brown's chancellorship and premiership, the gravamen of the criticism is that he nailed his colours to the mast labelled 'light touch regulation'. At first, as noted, he was widely praised for his 1997 reforms in which decision-making over interest rates was granted to the Bank of England and responsibility for banking supervision was taken away.

There were few hostile critics of this reform; yet, when the storm broke, and the banking system had to be rescued by the government, with a major impact on the government's tax revenues, it was Gordon Brown who got the blame. "I know I have to take the rap," he told me on one occasion, before going on to point out that the economy was actually recovering perceptibly, if not dramatically, when he was voted out of office.

The other candidate to be metaphorically pelted in the stocks was the governor of the Bank of England, Sir Mervyn King, for having also adopted a light touch approach to regulation. For, although supervision had been formally removed from the Bank, it was still charged with responsibility for 'financial stability', and financial stability is most certainly not a phrase that sits easily with the course of events in financial markets on the latter part of the governor's watch.

There was nothing new about the Bank of England as an institution favouring light touch regulation. It was light touch regulation that lay behind the Bank's failure to spot and act upon the problems at Johnson Matthey Bankers in 1984 – a failure the memory of which was one of the reasons why Brown was keen to remove formal supervision from the Bank in 1997, the other being the collapse of BCCI in 1991, about which the then governor, Robin Leigh-Pemberton, rather rashly remarked: "It is not the task of regulators to prevent financial institutions from making lending mistakes."

As Marjorie Dean and Robert Pringle have written: "Supervision is a big yawn until things go wrong…when the Bank of England closed the corrupt Bank of Credit and Commerce International in London in July 1991, indignant voices were heard asking for the regulatory and monetary functions in Britain to be officially divided, the implication being that because the central bank gives too much attention to the latter to the detriment of the former, it had failed to spot irregularities at BCCI as soon as it should have done."

As it turned out, separation of the regulatory and monetary functions, when it finally came in 1997, was not a happy divorce. Subsequent experience demonstrated that the former partners ought to have kept in closer touch, and that personal relationships mattered.

The British public, and the political press that served it, thought of Gordon Brown's chancellorship and premiership almost entirely in domestic terms. This was hardly surprising. In democracies, politics, like charity, begins at home. But throughout the period that he was at first lauded for his achievements and later criticised for his perceived failure to eliminate 'boom and bust', Brown maintained a passionate interest in international economic affairs – an interest that served him well when it came to the onset of the financial crisis in 2007-09.

With his background in history, Brown knew all about the way that the International Monetary Fund was set up after the Bretton Woods Conference in 1944 to be one of the key institutions. Their primary purpose was to ensure that the world economy progressed on a more even keel than it had in the 1920s and 1930s, with all that the failure of economic policy in those years entailed – not least in the sphere of coordination of policy.

Brown was sufficiently interested in the work of the IMF to take seriously an enquiry in 1999 as to whether he would consider leaving the Treasury and becoming the first British managing director at the IMF. Having fought so long in opposition to become chancellor, and with his sights set on eventually moving next door to No. 10, Brown would have surprised many of his supporters if he had abandoned it all for what was essentially a bureaucratic post, albeit a very distinguished one. Yet he took the 'sounding out' process sufficiently seriously to make tentative enquiries with other European finance ministers as to whether they would support his candidacy.

In the end he decided against, and proceeded to become the longest-serving chancellor since Sir Nicholas Vansittart. He was also, for a long time, lauded from all sides, including by what were always likely to prove fair-weather friends in the Conservative press. But, as noted, an IMF function that he did agree to accept, and a post which he held for many years, was the chairmanship of its key policymaking committee, the International Monetary and Finance Committee (IMFC) which met twice a year, at the official annual IMF meeting in the autumn, and the lower-key meeting in the spring.

Notes, references and further reading:

1) The Central Banks, Marjorie Dean & Robert Pringle, 1994.

CHAPTER 6

A JOB TURNED DOWN– WITH
HISTORIC CONSEQUENCES

THE BRITISH, in the shape of John Maynard Keynes and a high-powered array of his fellow British economists, had played a decisive role in the formation of the IMF – although not, in the view of Keynes then and Brown many decades later, decisive enough. The manifestly more powerful US negotiators had ruled out Keynes's idea of making the IMF into a kind of world central bank, and had not been prepared to allow symmetrical arrangements under which countries in balance of payments surplus should be as obliged to reduce their surpluses as deficit countries were to eliminate their deficits.

As a Labour chancellor, Gordon Brown was all too conscious of the problems his predecessors had had with the IMF – both under the Wilson governments of 1964-70 and the Callaghan regime of 1976-79. Indeed, the humiliation of the Callaghan government having to go cap in hand to the IMF in 1976 was one about which Labour was taunted by the Conservatives for many years. Even now, nearly 40 years later, memories are revived of Denis Healey, the chancellor of the time, having to 'turn back at the airport' because the pressing business of the UK's domestic economic crisis forced him to face the music at home, and not attend the annual jamboree, which that year was in Manila. Such was the state of the Labour Party's

31

constitution at the time that Healey, the chancellor and very senior member of the Cabinet, had to address the Labour Party conference that week from the floor of the conference, and not the platform.

However, after some difficult months, and fractious Cabinet meetings, Callaghan and Healey managed to negotiate the loan and keep the Cabinet together. The time when the government could repay the loan was christened by Healey "sod off day". And after that the chancellor spent a year as chairman of the key policymaking committee, a role which many years later, would fall into the lap of one Gordon Brown.

But not just for 12 months, which for many years since the 1970s was the usual tenure for the chairmanship of the IMF's political committee. The IMFC evolved from something called the Interim Committee – a committee which itself derived from the work of another Englishman, the banker Sir Jeremy Morse, who after the demise of the Bretton Woods exchange rate system in 1971-73, was charged with devising a new set of rules for international monetary cooperation, in the hope that something more formal could be salvaged from the rather chaotic scene known as 'benign neglect' – the era when the US government in Washington, under President Nixon and after, drew back from its earlier responsibilities for the system.

This era of benign neglect is important to our story, because it was principally in reaction to US policy of the time that Chancellor Helmut Schmidt of West Germany and President Valéry Giscard d'Estaing of France inaugurated the European Monetary System, which was to cause so much internal agony to both major British political parties, and to be developed into the European Single Currency. Given what they regarded as the international monetary disorder of the 1970s, what Schmidt and Giscard wanted was 'a zone of monetary stability' within Europe. In the light of the disorder in the eurozone that followed the onset of the financial crisis in 2007-08, the outcome of the Schmidt-Giscard strategy has turned out to be somewhat ironic.

Gordon Brown's 'five tests' and the issue of whether or not Britain should sign up for the single currency played a dominant role in the Blair government's first two terms. It is interesting to speculate what would have happened if Brown had departed the London scene for that full-time job as managing director of the IMF in 1999. I have never been especially interested in such 'what if' and 'if only' questions; but it seems very probable that, in the absence of Brown, Tony Blair would have got his way, and Britain would have joined the eurozone, thereby inhibiting the flexibility of its economic policy when it came to the Great Recession.

In other words, by not taking that job Gordon Brown made a not insignificant contribution to the course of Britain's destiny. And, by taking, and managing to hold on for eight years – against all historical precedents – Brown managed to be at the forefront of the international economic and financial debate in the run-up to the financial crisis. What was more, as an assiduous networker, with seemingly boundless energy and enthusiasm for the one-to-one meeting or phone call, Brown had managed to build up an extremely impressive and enviable range of contacts both in the US and Continental Europe, so that, during the crucial years of 2008-09, and in particular during the preparations for and conduct of the G20 meeting in London, April 2009, Brown was the best placed leader in the universe to 'save the world.'

For many years Labour leaders had been making speeches about international economic and financial matters, which, to their consternation, attracted little attention. I recall John Smith's economic adviser telephoning me during the late 1980s and pleading: "Please, please, can somebody find space to report something about John's speech on the IMF."

As chancellor, Gordon Brown attended the annual meetings of the World Bank and IMF in Hong Kong in September 1997, just a few months after the general election, and in the wake of the Asian financial crisis. The economic and social devastation in countries such as Thailand and Indonesia made a big impression on him. Looking back in 2010 on the Asian crisis Brown saw the roots of both the subsequent banking crisis of 2007 onwards and the problems of growing imbalances in the world trading system.

As far back as 15 December 1998, he delivered a major speech at Harvard University in which he called for nothing less than a fully-fledged system of "global financial regulation". This should deal with imbalances caused by the kind of global capital flows that simply did not exist on anything like the modern scale under the Bretton Woods system of very limited capital movements. Even then, long before Mervyn King, as governor of the Bank of England, became known for his concerns about 'moral hazard', Brown was urging that policymakers should "minimise the risks arising from insider information on the one hand and moral hazard on the other."

There is an abundance of written evidence that, in his own words, Brown "fought internationally post-Asia for a proper monitoring of risk and an early warning system." However, there is also no shortage of evidence that, again in his own words, "I had to accept that I had lost the argument and that the best we had been able to achieve was a Financial Stability Forum with responsibility for, but little power over, financial stability."

Brown is also quite open about the mistake he made in going along with the general consensus, associated, as noted, especially with his friend Alan Greenspan, that the sophistication of modern financial markets had reduced the dangers of a crisis. Thus, while acknowledging that there was an historical tendency for credit booms to occur and conceding "We also knew that at the peak of a cycle extra capital will be needed when there are greater risks in the system," he freely admits: "Of course with a leveraged economy, there would always be risk. But I and others felt that, if there was a diversification of risk spread across many institutions and through many instruments, we were in a better position."

One sometimes gets the impression that the Cameron-Osborne government blames Brown for the entire world financial crash, just as they like to make out that Labour's lax budgetary policies were responsible for almost all of the deterioration in the government's finances. The truth is that Brown was one of hundreds of western policymakers who succumbed to the conventional wisdom about the self-righting qualities of the financial markets, and the Labour government's public spending plans were responsible for only a small part of the deterioration in the budgetary position. Moreover, just as Labour had backed Kenneth Clarke's plans for a two-year freeze on public spending in the late 1990s, so Cameron and Osborne were vociferously backing Labour's public spending plans of the mid to late 2000-2010 decade.

It did not help Brown's case that he had made that rash promise that there would be no more boom and bust, especially since, as an historian, he was well aware of power of the credit cycle.

There was ambivalence in Brown's thinking. He knew there was insufficient regulation, yet he was trying to convince himself that the markets were indeed self-correcting. Like his hero Alan Greenspan, Brown was "assuming that risk had indeed been dispersed across the system." The reasoning? "The very new, very diverse range of institutions and instruments implied that the failure of one institution did not necessarily lead to the failure of some or all. But the world of finance was operating without the benefit of the global financial oversight I had been pressing for – and also without any comprehensive global picture of the full scale of the shadow and formal activities of the financial institutions and of their entanglements with each other."

That diversification of risk provided reassurance was, Brown now believes, "the biggest and most far-reaching mistake I and others made." Excessive leverage – too much debt, too much lending in relation to capital – may have been one of the roots of the problem. Yet Brown, a socialist, believes that "modern capitalism needs leverage to flourish." The obsession shared by Brown and other G7 policymakers was the battle against high inflation – the cause of most recessions since the Second World War. It was, as we have seen, the granting of independence to the Bank of England to fight inflation via 'inflation targeting' that won such plaudits for Brown in the early years of his chancellorship. But it was the fact that the Bank of England devoted far more resources to the battle against inflation than to its other brief, 'financial stability', that contributed to the failures of supervision which began with Northern Rock in August 2007 and then spread a lot further.

When the Northern Rock crisis broke, the UK monetary authorities were caught off guard, even though there had been something very suspicious about the way Northern Rock had been operating. I vividly recall how our own household was examining remortgage plans, and my wife, a commercial barrister, took one look at the way Northern Rock was extending itself and smelt a rat. And the FSA had warned the Treasury and the Bank a month earlier about its concerns.

The Treasury and the Bank of England were hit by the Rock affair within months of the handover from Tony Blair to Gordon Brown. Brown had asked Alistair Darling to be his chancellor: Darling was an old friend, and regarded as a safe pair of hands. Somehow or other, in previous assignments such as at the Department of Transport, Darling had avoided the kind of adverse publicity that is often associated with such departments. Indeed, one of Darling's quiet achievements at Transport was that, thanks to his good relations with chancellor Brown at the time, he managed to resist a plan by Treasury officials to pull down St Pancras Station – the renovation of which has proved one of the most outstanding architectural contributions to modern London, and a happy home to the relocated Eurostar terminal.

In his instant memoir 'Back from the Brink' Darling almost disarmingly refers to the fact that it was he himself who was largely responsible for the 'architecture' of the FSA as well, having been shadow minister for the City during the run-up to the 1997 election, when Brown was planning his big shake-up of the Bank of England.

Neither Brown nor Darling was responsible for the way that the US sub-prime crisis and the bursting of the US housing bubble led to the onset of the Bear Stearns crisis on 17 July 2007, with repercussions in Europe – the first sign of which was the freezing of three of its investment funds by the French investment bank BNP Paribas on 9 August. But what the management of Northern Rock was responsible for was excessive dependence on short-term money market financing, and that source of funds simply came to an end when the financial markets dried up that August, because nobody trusted anybody, not least because they suspected – often rightly – that if their own books were in a bad state then so were those of other financial institutions.

In reaction to the Bear Stearns and BNP Paribas crises the US Federal Reserve and the European Central Bank (ECB) were quick off the mark in pumping liquidity into the system, but for Northern Rock the game was up. Darling discovered that, although he had been alerted to the problems at Northern Rock on 14 August, the FSA had been aware of Northern Rock's excessive dependence on short-term money markets funds, as opposed to savers' deposits, since February 2007. And it was not only short-term finance: it was short-term finance from the US, the home, as it were, of the sub-prime market associated with the US real estate bubble.

Oddly enough, Gordon Brown himself, both as chancellor and as an (early days) prime minister, appears to have shown

37

more interest in the deficiencies of the international regulatory structure than the domestic one, which latter he fancied he had put on a sound basis with his tripartite structure.

However, as Darling notes, "the system depended on a strong working relationship between the FSA and the Bank of England." By choosing Sir Howard Davies, direct from his position as deputy governor of the Bank, to be the first head of the FSA in 1997, Brown no doubt thought he had laid the groundwork for such a good relationship. But Howard Davies is a man who has always moved on in his career, and by the time the financial crisis broke in summer 2007, the chairman was Callum McCarthy. From what I have learned from the City, Whitehall and Bank of England insiders, Alistair Darling was, if anything, using understatement when he described the relationship between Bank governor Mervyn King and FSA chairman Callum McCarthy as "often strained, at times prickly."

Brown has been widely blamed for the putatively faulty structure of the seemingly 'divide and rule' tripartite structure. But the more I have talked to close observers of the scene, the more it has appeared that the problem lay less with the structure than with the interaction between the personalities. This was certainly a problem during the early days of the Northern Rock affair. Prime minister Brown and governor King were strong, dominant personalities with entrenched positions. On later occasions, the two were united, however, in going behind the chancellor's back.

The handling of the Northern Rock affair was not helped by the combination of the entrenched positions of prime minister and governor, and a defect in the regulatory structure – his own regulatory structure! – discovered by chancellor Darling. And the cat was put among the pigeons by the energetic and well-informed BBC business editor, Robert Peston, who broke the story of the rescue plan the night before the planned announcement and who was therefore blamed for the panic queues outside the offices of Northern Rock – pictures of which were flashed around the world. I myself was present shortly afterwards at a monetary seminar in Washington, where the former US Federal Reserve chairman Paul Volcker wryly observed that things had come to a pretty pass when the world watched queues forming outside what was for Volcker and others and a faraway financial institution of which they knew little. And yet, even if the 'business model' of the faulty ship Northern Rock had been bound to run aground eventually, the timing of that particular shipwreck was indubitably precipitated by the repercussions from the sub-prime crisis, repercussions already felt by Bear Stearns and BNP Paribas.

It was patently obvious at the time, even to such right-wing veterans as Nigel Lawson, who might in theory be ideologically opposed to nationalisation, that immediate nationalisation of Northern Rock was probably necessary. But, ironically, Gordon Brown, who had in his youth been drawn ideologically to nationalisation, had a serious hang-up about it. Had not the Labour Party spent years, indeed decades, distancing itself from its belief in state ownership and proclaiming its embrace of the wonders of market economics? Had not Tony Blair, in a celebrated speech to the annual Labour Party Conference, finally announced the abandonment of Clause Four of the Labour Party's constitution – the clause, long since honoured only in theory, that committed the Party to the common ownership of the "means of production, distribution and exchange"?

Here was the moment, the onset of the crisis of 'finance capitalism' about which the youthful Gordon Brown and his folk hero the independent Labour MP James Maxton (about whom Brown had written a biography) had dreamed. In Brown's words: "After addressing the most obvious sign of the crisis [giving guarantees for depositors to quell the public panic] we next had to look for the solution to the problem of a failed British bank. Here I intervened. I was against nationalisation, especially of a failed bank, and at that stage I would not let it be considered."

Brown favoured a private sector solution, "partly because, ever since the 1970s, the Labour Party had been losing elections on the question of economic competence." Again: "Tony Blair and I had spent twenty years building New Labour on the foundation of market competition, private enterprise, and economic stability as the path to growth and I was not prepared to undermine that painstaking work with one instant decision."

The governor, Mervyn King, had no particular hang-ups about Labour's history. He had, when deputy governor, been closely consulted by the Brown, Darling, Balls team about Labour's plans for monetary and financial stability, and he had come to the job as one of the brightest academic economists of his generation. What concerned him, and he went on about this long after the dramatic weekend of the initial crisis of Northern Rock, was the concept, and danger, of what economists and philosophers call moral hazard – the danger that, if banks know that in the end they will be rescued by the state, then they have an incentive to take excessive risks. Even as I write, five years later in the summer of 2012, this problem of moral hazard still looms over all efforts at regulatory reform and good governance.

In his memoir, Darling complains bitterly about his problems in dealing with Mervyn King. Mervyn King, in turn, had problems dealing with Alistair Darling. But Darling's shocked discovery in the preceding week was that he could not order King to provide the degree of liquidity support to the market that the Federal Reserve and ECB had done earlier. "I asked Treasury officials if there was a way of forcing the governor's hand." The answer was "No." As Darling ruefully commented: "The fact that we had given the Bank independence had a downside as well as an upside."

For Darling, the general state of dilatoriness and confusion regarding Northern Rock reflected something very simple and obvious: "The real problem was this: for ten years there had been no financial crisis." The Bank had focused principally on fighting inflation, in which battle for many years it was considered successful, and Gordon Brown had won praise all round for having granted so much independence to the Bank. The Bank appeared to be asleep on its watch when it came to financial stability and systemic risk. And the FSA had spotted something wrong with Northern Rock as early as February, but the concept of 'light touch' regulation was in the ascendancy, and Northern Rock continued to offer 100 per cent plus mortgages while relying excessively on the short-term money markets to finance them. Yet, who knows? If it had not been for the 'globalised' consequences of the sub-prime crisis, and the seizing up of the money markets that August and September, Northern Rock might have lasted a lot longer.

A sense of urgency about Northern Rock struck Darling, King and Callum McCarthy, at the beginning of September. Amazingly, they discovered that they did not possess the legal powers to take the bank over. The idea of Lloyds TSB coming to the rescue did not get very far. King was against massive injections of liquidity: "The provision of large liquidity penalises those financial institutions that sat out the dance, encourages herd behaviour and increases the intensity of future crises." Nevertheless it was agreed that the Bank would have to help out in its traditional capacity as 'lender of last resort', but the plan to announce this in the morning of Friday 14 September was, as noted, excitedly announced overnight by Robert Peston and general panic ensued. The panic was fomented by the fact that at the time there was not yet in existence a blanket guarantee about the safety of customers' deposits. This was finally announced on the Monday afternoon, both for Northern Rock and for any other bank failure. But the damage had been done. It was perfectly rational to queue to move one's savings, even if the sum total of such individual actions guaranteed the demise of the bank.

All the official participants were learning on the job. In King's view, the tripartite arrangement had worked perfectly well until things became very 'political' during the Northern Rock crisis. In the past the Bank of England had conducted many a 'covert' rescue operation – including assistance to individual manufacturing companies during the early 1980s, when the early Thatcherite monetarist policies were crucifying even good companies. King had wanted a 'covert' operation for Northern Rock, but the chancellor had vetoed this idea; times had changed, and it would probably be leaked – as, indeed, the plan for the covert 'lender of last resort' device was leaked.

The 'political' nature of the rescue operations that weekend is illustrated by disagreements between Treasury and Bank about precisely when King recommended assurance for depositors. Gordon Brown's concerns about the potential costs of deposit protection also delayed things, as he freely concedes. Yet when Brown was still chancellor he had asked Ed Balls, then City Minister to conduct a 'Britain-only simulation exercise' of what might happen in the event of a bank failure. Apparently most of those involved began the exercises with concerns about 'moral hazard'predominant, but ended acknowledging that rescues might be necessary. Brown, as subsequent events showed, was always interested in exploring a private sector solution; but, as he frankly admits, there were no private sector participants in the simulation exercise – oddly, when one considers his strong interest in, and propagation of, international regulation. Also, "there was no detailed discussion of the increased entanglement of institutions with each other..." It is therefore perhaps no surprise that when the crisis came there was, in the initial stages, confusion confounded, and much mud-slinging and attribution of blame.

Now, although the legislation was not in place for a public takeover, all is fair in war and financial crises, and it was most certainly open to the prime minister to act dramatically. It is clear that Gordon Brown considered nationalisation, whatever the legal position – there is such a thing, after all, as emergency legislation; there are 'emergency powers' – but, as already noted, he was against nationalisation for reasons to do with the Labour Party's history and its concerns about economic competence. It is therefore an unfortunate twist of fate, and most certainly an unintended consequence, that one observer could write: "The chaos on 17 September was the moment that Labour's reputation for economic competence vanished ... the government's 'Black Wednesday' moment."

Notes, references and further reading:

1) The story about Brown's interest in the IMF job in 1999 did not come from the Brown camp, but from a Continental European diplomatist who could hardly believe that the Chancellor of the Exchequer could possibly be even considering such a move.

2) The IMF episode of 1976 dominated the second half of that year. It is referred to in the then Chancellor Denis Healey's memoirs, *The Time of My Life* (1989), and the then Prime Minister James Callaghan's memoirs *Time and Chance* (1987). Lord Healey, to this day, believes the Government need not have had to depend on the IMF if the Treasury's statistics and forecasts had been accurate- a point which is disputed by Sir Douglas Wass, who was Treasury Permanent Secretary at the time, in his detailed insider account of the 1976 crisis, "Decline to Fall." (2008). Callaghan makes it clear that the speech in which he said that the days were gone when a country could spend its way out of recession was tactical, and that, fundamentally, he still believed in Keynesian expansionary policies in time of recession.

3) Many of the quotations from Gordon Brown in this and subsequent chapters are not 'private information' but taken from his book *Beyond The Crash*, 2010. This is a work that was largely ignored at the time, but which is an invaluable contribution to understanding the period, and on which I have drawn copiously.

4) An important ally of Schmidt's and Giscard's was Roy Jenkins, who had temporarily retired from the British political scene to become President of the European Commission.

5) The five economic tests to be passed (or failed) concerned: First, whether there could be "sustainable convergence" between Britain and the others. Secondly, whether there was "sufficient flexibility" to cope with economic change. Thirdly, the effect on investment. Fourthly, the impact on Britain's financial services. And, lastly, whether membership of the single currency would be "good for employment." The eventual study comprised 19 volumes totalling 6,000 pages. The essential

message was that adopting a "one size fits all" policy for interest rates would be a huge mistake, and losing exchange rate flexibility would be a disaster. It was all foreshadowed in the various speeches and lectures by Ed Balls on the mistakes made in the past by adhering to an overvalued exchange rate.

6) Alistair Darling reveals the story behind the preservation of St Pancras Station in his very readable and informative memoir Back From The Brink, 2010. Given the extremely bad relations at times between most of the key participants in the handling of the financial crisis, his "instant" memoir is a case of "getting one's retaliation in first." I draw on Darling's account in the rest of this monograph. Among other things, his hostility towards Bank Governor, Sir Mervyn King has whetted appetites for any memoirs that might be forthcoming from the Governor in due course. But I also draw on what others have told me about Darling.

7) *In Banking On The Future*, 2010, Howard Davies and David Green also have some trenchant comments on the Governor's performance.

8) The allegation that the chaotic reaction to the Northern Rock crisis was the Brown government's "Black Wednesday" moment is in Brummer, op.cit.

9) See Mervyn King, letter to Treasury Committee 12 ix 2007

10) In evidence to the Public Accounts Committee about the privatisation of Northern Rock on 17 September 2012, Sir Nicholas Macpherson, permanent secretary to the Treasury, said : " With the benefit of hindsight the Treasury was slow off the mark in terms of addressing the problem..There was a five month period of drift . That made it quite likely we would lose money on Northern Rock." The whole episode was a " monumental collective failure, of which the Treasury was part."

CHAPTER 7

BETWEEN A ROCK AND

A HARD CHOICE

AFTER NORTHERN ROCK: the deluge! In the period immediately after 27 June, when he succeeded Tony Blair without so much as an internal Labour Party election, Gordon Brown had been a popular prime minister. This was partly because he was not Tony Blair, and not associated in the public mind with the invasion of Iraq. But it was also because in those early weeks, before the culmination of the Northern Rock crisis, he had generally been considered to handle things well. Within a short space of time there was a foiled terrorist attack, and two familiar British occurrences: floods, and an outbreak of foot and mouth disease. His reaction was calm and low-key, striking the right note. He seemed to behave in a way that was deliberately the opposite of Tony Blair's approach: for example, not reviving the rhetoric about the 'war on terror', and showing suitable concern about the floods, in contrast to David Cameron, who left his flooded constituency to proceed with a trip to Rwanda.

Although 'not being Blair' got the new prime minister safely through the first few weeks, it was not long before he was beginning to feel the strain. Blair had always feared that Brown was too obsessive and focused on particular issues to be able to cope with the manifold complications and interruptions of a modern prime minister's day. At the Treasury he was used to one big event to prepare for, namely the Budget, and various predictable public appearances. He had chosen his own agenda, and spent much of his time scheming to unseat Blair and become prime minister.

The popular impression is that, when he actually got there, Brown did not seem to have a plan. This was also the impression of people who worked quite close to him on Downing Street.

According to journalist Steve Richards, he did have a plan: to call a general election the following April, when he had settled in. But he could not resist trying to undermine the Conservatives and their relatively new leader David Cameron by allowing speculation to develop that he might call an election at any time. Such speculation got out of hand during the Party Conference season of early autumn 2007, and Brown was wrong-footed by a pledge from shadow chancellor George Osborne to reduce inheritance tax. He responded in a panic by instructing his chancellor Alistair Darling, fresh in the job, to retaliate by making Labour's own concessions on inheritance tax, to be financed, as Osborne had proposed, by a controversial tax on so called 'non-doms' – people working in London but not officially domiciled there.

This was one of many factors that contributed to the 'on-off' election decision – there were narrowing opinion polls in marginal constituencies, question marks over the state of readiness of Labour's election machine, and goodness knows how many other tortuous calculations. We shall never know what the result might have been if an election had indeed been called – there was a famous episode in 1978 when James Callaghan, having been in office rather longer than Brown was at 'indecision time', decided not to go ahead with an election in October 1978. Much mud was flung, and blame attributed; there was the unedifying spectacle of Brown's associates running for cover. But the general verdict was that Brown had 'bottled it', and from then on it was all downhill. Callaghan's government went through the notorious winter of discontent in 1978-79, and an election was due anyway in 1979. Brown carried on for three agonising years, depressed that he had made the wrong decision.

Yet, despite all the obloquy about Brown's personality, conduct and record on the domestic scene, it is my belief that, as events turned out, he was the right man, in the right place, at the right time for the onset of the international financial crisis. As I write in the summer of 2012, the western world's economy is by no means out of the woods. But at least Gordon Brown's initiatives stopped the rot.

The disgraced former managing director of the IMF, Dominique Strauss-Kahn, coined the phrase 'The Great Recession' to describe what hit the world in 2008-09. This was a deliberate attempt to contrast recent experience with that of the 1929-32 Great Depression, when output and employment fell far more drastically. There can be little doubt that Gordon Brown played a vital role in the bank recapitalisation moves not just in the UK, but also in the US and Continental Europe in the autumn of 2008 – a recapitalisation exercise that is generally agreed to have been a necessary, if not sufficient, condition for rescuing the economy from the brink of disaster.

That recapitalisation was necessary but not sufficient was illustrated in the first few months of 2009, when it is no exaggeration to say that world trade simply collapsed. The huge, concerted economic policy stimulus agreed under the auspices of the G20 was the 'other shoe' – an essential supplement to the recapitalisation of the banks. Gordon Brown's handling of bank recapitalisation vies with his successful conduct of the G20 meeting in London, April 2009 as his finest hour. Indeed, they were two fine hours. And there is an exquisite irony in the way that April 2009 had been the month when, if his original plan had gone ahead, Brown would have been preoccupied with a general election to win wider legitimacy for his premiership.

Notes, references and further reading:

1) In this and subsequent chapters I have drawn frequently on *Whatever It Takes – The Real Story of Gordon Brown and New Labour*, Steve Richards, 2010.

CHAPTER 8

THE CRISIS UNFOLDS

FOR THE BRITISH, Northern Rock was the first sign of crisis. The affair dragged on through the autumn and winter of 2007-08, and finally, on 17 February 2008, chancellor Darling announced that Northern Rock would be 'temporarily' taken into public ownership, i.e. nationalised. Basically, what happened in those months was that Gordon Brown's attention was being devoted increasingly to the international crisis. American banks were announcing a stream of losses connected with the sub-prime affair, and, as Brown says: "By December, it was becoming clear that the sub-prime crisis was having a major impact on the willingness of banks to lend to each other." The Federal Reserve, the ECB, the Bank of England, plus the central banks of Switzerland and Canada, were coordinating, pushing billions of dollars of liquidity into the system, in the hope of defrosting the financial markets. Brown's first Christmas in Scotland as prime minister with his family was not, on his own admission, relaxing. He was fretting about the international financial situation, and not agreeing with those commentators who were arguing that the pressures were beginning to ease.

Brown shared his concerns with the annual gathering of members of the World Economic Forum in Davos, January 2008, warning that the scale of banks' losses threatened recession, that banking regulation had to be tightened – end of New

Labour's flirtation with the soft touch! – and that bold fiscal and monetary policies would be required.

On return to the UK he headed a meeting of European members of the G8 annual 'summiteers', which he had called in London. This was an important foundation for a continual interchange between Brown, Chancellor Merkel of Germany and President Sarkozy of France over the next 2½ years, as well as with European Commission President Jose Manuel Barroso. The socialist Italian prime minister Romano Prodi was at this meeting, but on his way out of office, yielding to Silvio Berlusconi.

This was the beginning of a regular series of meetings, telephone calls and video-conferences as the crisis developed. But at this stage Brown had to acknowledge that, although he had sown the seeds of his view that this was not just an American crisis, "I sensed that even now my European colleagues believed this was America's crisis alone, and that the UK was affected because it has the same Anglo-Saxon financial system. They were not alone in hoping that the rest of Europe might escape the worst of the crisis."

While Brown's domestic premiership rapidly seemed to lose its sense of purpose, and stories about bad temper and petulance were rife, he continued to be focused principally on the international financial crisis. He spoke to President George W. Bush early in February 2008 about the possibility of a "more effective joint plan to reduce marketplace uncertainty" and the following weekend Alistair Darling and the G7 finance ministers called for prompt disclosure of bank losses. At that stage, Brown was hoping that the mere declaration of losses would restore trust and confidence in the interbank market and hence ensure normal services for retail bank lending. But this was rather a forlorn hope. "There was to be a slow but gradually dawning realisation that the [bank] assets were so impaired and the losses so great that the banks did not actually have enough capital to declare these losses."

Meanwhile, the Treasury was going through the motions of considering various private sector solutions to the Northern Rock crisis, before facing up to the inevitability of nationalisation. Darling says that he and the prime minister with whom he frequently clashed were nevertheless "in the same place on Northern Rock." For Brown, however, "I accepted with an incredibly heavy heart the reality of the choice the Treasury presented me with." Moreover he had no idea that "six months later I would be the one initiating the government's buying into the biggest banks in the country."

The youthful would-be nationaliser had got over the hang-up induced by Mrs Thatcher and the electoral unpopularity of nationalisation, and was now going to have to nationalise, or partly nationalise banks left, right and centre. But it was to be eight months of mounting concern before the dramatic announcement of the government taking significant stakes in Royal Bank of Scotland, HBOS and Lloyds TSB.

Brown was particularly struck by the announcement across the Atlantic on 14 March 2008 that Bear Stearns, worth $18 billion a year earlier, was being acquired by JP Morgan Chase for a mere $240 million. He emphasised his concerns to President Sarkozy in a meeting at No. 10 on 27 March, and the two issued a statement calling for "greater transparency in financial markets to ensure that banks make full and prompt disclosure of the scale of write-offs." On 8 April he was shocked by the release of the IMF's calculation that aggregate potential losses stemming from the sub-prime crisis could reach $945 billion, equivalent to some 7 per cent of US gross domestic product.

The ramifications of the sub-prime crisis reached the mortgage market in Britain, and Brown now became interested in the liquidity and funding of building societies. The Treasury commissioned Sir James Crosby, deputy chairman of the FSA, to report on ways of improving the functioning of mortgage markets. Brown says: "I was very supportive because I knew that unless we could get the mortgage market lending again, we were heading for a major recession if not worse."

By the time of the G7 and IMF spring meetings in Washington on 11 and 12 April 2008, the British were worried that the US monetary authorities were not facing up to the size of problems revealed by the IMF's report of potential losses. It was not necessarily a problem of liquidity. Mervyn King, after a long period when he was widely criticised by prime minister, Treasury and even some colleagues for his obsession with 'moral hazard' and his perceived slowness to grasp the seriousness of the banking crisis, was now making up for lost time.

On Monday 17 March, the very same day that JP Morgan had bought Bear Stearns for a song, King revealed to a lunch hosted by the American Ambassador to London that he saw "Two imperatives": one, to tide the banks over the short-term confidence problem via what became know, after joint work with the Treasury, as the 'Special Liquidity Scheme' (SLS), unveiled on 21 April. (This turned out to be needed even more than was at first calculated, with a 'take-up' of $185 billion, almost four times the original calculation.)

Second, King saw the need for, in the words of Ambassador Tuttle's cable back to Washington, "a coordinated effort to possibly recapitalise the global banking system." This was an early indication that Brown and King were beginning to come together in their analytical approach to the crisis. The months following the onset of the Northern Rock crisis in August 2007 had seen some of the worst periods of bad relations between Downing Street and the Bank of England for many a year. The governor had been so unpopular that both Brown and Darling had been reluctant to reappoint him. But they decided that they had no better candidate, and it was easier to stick with the devil they knew. King, for his part, if he had decided to depart from the fray – which must have been tempting – would have been left with a nagging feeling that he had not seen the crisis through.

As far as Gordon Brown and Alistair Darling were concerned, King's discovery of the liquidity problem had come rather late in the day. Writing of the aftermath of the August 2007 Northern Rock crisis, Darling says: "Mervyn's analysis was that the underlying problem was that banks did not have enough capital. In that he was right. But he did not accept that there was a second problem, a much more immediate one, which was lack of liquidity – that is, the banks' reluctance to lend to one another. That was what happened with Northern Rock and I did not want it to happen to another bank, let alone to the banking system as a whole."

Darling records how, just before Christmas, King told him that he now recognised the liquidity problem, and that he regretted having not confronted the issue before, when on his 'moral hazard' high horse. The way Darling phrases the next point is intriguing: he says that King recognised that "it wasn't just the lack of capital that was the problem."

The 'just' is poignant, because it was the spreading of the message to the wider world that re-capitalisation was needed that became Gordon Brown's mission in the autumn of 2008. The 'problem' lay with both liquidity and solvency. It was all very well recognising the capital problem, but the liquidity issue had to be dealt with first. The two issues were not mutually exclusive. But, although King had recognised the solvency aspect first, it was Gordon Brown who was eventually to seize the political initiative, seeing the need for recapitalising the UK banks and spreading the word to Washington as well.

Notes, references and further reading:

1) There are many references to bank "capital" from hereon. The essential point is the growing concern about whether a bank's "assets" are worth what they are supposed to be, in the light of the collapse in the value of those of its customers' "assets", against which loans were made. An institution is deemed insolvent if its liabilities outweigh its assets, and it cannot repay its debts. An institution that is fundamentally sound may suffer a temporary liquidity problem, which can be cured if it

raises enough money from selling some assets, or even becomes more efficient at debt collection.

2) The exchanges between the Governor and the American ambassador are covered in *The Bank*, Dan Conaghan, 2012.

CHAPTER 9

YOU CANNOT BANK ON BANKS .....

WHILE THE MAGNITUDE of the financial crisis was dawning on Brown in those first months of 2008 he was having regular video conferences with George W. Bush, visited the US President in April at the White House, met the presidential candidates from whom Bush's successor was going to emerge, and gave the Kennedy Lecture in Boston, where he called for a "declaration of interdependence". Under this, in his own words, there would be "far greater international coordination for dealing with exactly the problems we were facing; this included cooperation on dealing with bank failures as well as coordination of economic policies."

When he returned to London he summoned British bank chiefs together on 15 April, and was struck by the way that most of them wanted greater provision of official liquidity "but there seemed to be very little self analysis of their problems and only limited focus on the broader issue of lending to the wider economy." The prime minister and former chancellor retained his eye for the key economic statistics and "lending by banks [i.e. lack of it] was rapidly becoming my obsession."

What was becoming the Brown-King view that the issue might indeed be one of solvency seemed to gather further strength when there was, in April to June, a stream of rights issues from the Royal Bank of Scotland, HBOS and Barclays, totalling £20 billion, of which the RBS component was £12 billion – the biggest rights issue in British history.

Brown admits that he had made the mistake of thinking the banks were at last coming clean, raising the prospect of restoring normal service. "I was worried it was too late. That the biggest rights issue in British history was simply not enough was simply mind-bending." Meanwhile, the Great Recession was beginning: in 2008 UK GDP fell by 1 per cent, after a 3.6 per cent rise in 2007. And the man who had been fêted for granting independence to the Bank of England was fretting that interest rates were not falling fast enough in the face of the economic slowdown. The Bank's monetary policy committee did not change the bank rate between 10 April and 8 October, and the man who had granted their independence was powerless to do anything about it.

Summer 2008 was not a good one for a British prime minister who, while continually under pressure for lack of domestic vision, and now the object of would-be plots himself – after all those years plotting to unseat Blair – was increasingly preoccupied with the financial crisis. In the US the fall-out from the sub-prime crisis had hit the home loans institutions known as Fannie Mae and Freddie Mac; in Britain there had been an annual fall of almost a third in mortgage lending. Talk about boom and bust! The coiner of the phrase that had promised no more boom and bust said: "These figures made my blood run cold. I knew what they meant; people and businesses stuck without credit and possibly a bad recession ... the removal of credit was happening very suddenly ... I had expected to push and nudge the system back to order, but it was not happening."

It became clear in late July 2008 that the bank rights issues had not succeeded in stabilising the system. The Brown family took a much-publicised holiday in Southwold, Suffolk, but for the prime minister it was the equivalent of a busman's holiday. "The collapse in credit and its consequences for Britain's and the global economy was the question that obsessed me throughout our summer holiday." The man who found it difficult to cope as prime minister with a diary full of meetings that had not necessarily got anything to do with his main obsession was free to read widely: "It was then that I picked up and read Ben Bernanke's essays on the Great Depression."

Brown called upon his adviser Shriti Vadera to visit him, and they discussed Bernanke's ideas for what became known as 'quantitative easing'. This is basically a new term for the traditional practice of central bank 'open market operations', which involve measures to expand or shrink the supply of money and credit, the lesson of the Great Depression in the US being that the collapse of credit had been disastrous, and not counteracted by the Federal Reserve. Quantitative easing, or QE, became the fashion in the US and UK later, and is still with us as I write. But even its practitioners have trouble in explaining how effective it is, the main message being that it prevents things from being an awful lot worse.

Brown and Vadera decided that the failure of the bank rights issues indicated not only that the banks needed more capital but also that the markets suspected the banks were either not being honest about their losses or did not even know them.

The period when the British and other industrial economies looked like 'falling off a cliff' was the first three months of 2009, which made the principal contribution to the remarkable 14.4 per cent plunge in industrial production in the G7 group. But the rot was setting in during 2008, hence Brown's justified obsession with the state of the banking system and the world economy, while the newspapers were full of rumblings about his leadership, and rivals were plotting against the ace plotter.

With banks not lending and economic activity slowing Brown observed: "The more I explored the lessons from the past and cross-referenced them with the data from the present, the more it became clear that a huge fiscal stimulus and substantial quantitative easing would both be necessary." There

was a rider, reflecting his years of schooling in finance ministers' meetings and his experience as chairman of the IMF's key
policy committee of which, incidentally, for all the criticisms
of Brown's chaotic domestic premiership, one permanent IMF
official told me: "Your chancellor comes into the room with
a pile of seemingly disordered papers, looking disorganised
himself, and then proceeds to conduct a superbly businesslike
meeting."

The rider was fear that the stimulus could only work if the
rest of the world joined in. If it did not, then the UK would be
isolated and subject to attacks from the very financial markets
that had caused the trouble – just as individual eurozone countries like Greece were to be 'picked off' later. Also, and very
important from an economist's point of view, the cumulative
impact of a concerted effort would bring 'multiplier' benefits
that one country's expansion effort could not effect in isolation.

Later, on 29 August, there was one of many occasions for a
rift between Brown and his chancellor. Alistair Darling gave
what became a celebrated interview to Decca Aitkenhead of
the *Guardian*, in which he caused little short of a sensation by
saying that the economic outlook was "arguably the worst …
in sixty years."

This was not an interview celebrated by Gordon Brown,
whose reaction has been quoted elsewhere without the deletion
of expletives. One of Brown's aides said Brown's explosive reaction was not because he disagreed – he did not – but because
Darling's remarks were bound to hit confidence – "and he was
probably talking having spoken to Gordon."

However, fiscal and monetary stimulus, while a necessary
condition, was not sufficient. Shriti Vadera and the senior
Treasury official Tom Scholar both recall a 'defining moment'
when Scholar was crossing Trafalgar Square that summer and
took a call from Vadera and they both had a 'eureka' experience:
"it's capital". There had been other proposals for the mortgage

market, but both came to the conclusion that the immediate priority was indeed bank recapitalisation.

The big preoccupation of policy in the next few months was the recapitalisation of the British banks. Thanks to the close links and trust that had been built up by Brown abroad – unlike at home – he was able to play the key role also in persuading the Bush administration that recapitalisation was a necessity. Then he was the mastermind behind the $1 trillion stimulus announced in April 2009 at the London G20 summit.

Notes, references and further reading:

1) In this and subsequent chapters I have drawn on the exhaustive study Brown At 10, Anthony Seldon and Guy Lodge, 2010, as well as on background conversations with key officials.

2) Re fiscal action and "multiplier" benefits. The concept of the "multiplier" was the brainchild of the Cambridge economist Richard Kahn, an associate of Keynes.

The idea was that an initial boost of public spending, on, say, an infrastructure project, would have "multiplier" effects : workers being employed as a result would spend on other goods and services, thereby creating more employment, and contractors would create more employment via additional demand on their suppliers. In the kind of Great Recession we have experienced in recent years, the reverse happens, which is which is why premature cutbacks in public spending introduced by the Coalition under Chancellor Osborne have had such a pernicious effect.

CHAPTER 10

A SOCIALIST RIDES TO THE
RESCUE OF CAPITALISM

THE FINANCIAL CRISIS intensified after the 2008 August holiday. The troubled US mortgage firms Fannie Mae and Freddie Mac were nationalised on 7 September; Lehman Brothers unveiled large losses on 10 September and filed for bankruptcy on 15 September. This was an event that shook not only the financial world but the average lay-person, and is still spoken of as a signpost in the build-up of the world financial crisis. The US Treasury Secretary actually appealed to the UK for help, but as Alistair Darling has pointed out: "I had kept Gordon in touch. We were agreed that there was no way our government could effectively bankroll an American bank that was in trouble, when the US authorities wouldn't and when other US banks were running a mile." On the following day the US Federal Reserve took an 80 per cent stake in AIG, America's largest insurance company. The next day competition rules were waived for the go-ahead of a takeover by Lloyds TSB of HBOS. The myth spread that this was all fixed up by Brown and Sir Victor Blank of Lloyds over a drink. In fact, negotiations had been going on for some time, and the Treasury, Business Department, Bank of England and FSA all agreed, after much agonising, that in the circumstances this was the best option.

Brown and Darling understandably did not wish to get involved in a rescue of Lehman's that Washington could not contemplate. But Brown know that he still needed US support for his plans to save the banking system. On 25 September he addressed the UN in New York about the importance of one of his favourite missions, the Millennium Development goals (MDGs), arguing that the prevailing financial turbulence should not divert the UN from its plans to raise food production, eliminate malaria and improve education. In which context it is interesting that, after his fall from grace in the UK, he should have accepted a high-powered role from the UN in July 2012 to become the UN Special Envoy on education. From childhood Brown had adopted from his father, a Church of Scotland Minister, a deeply felt belief in the importance of helping the disadvantaged.

The UN speaking engagement had been fixed well before the escalation of the financial crisis, but the visit to New York afforded Brown and his team the opportunity to develop their plans, first with important discussions in New York and then a hastily arranged trip to see President Bush in the White House. The day after the announcement of the Lloyds TSB/HBOS deal, the Americans had unveiled their TARP (Troubled Assets Relief Program) scheme, aimed at seeking Congressional approval for the purchase of bank assets, but saying nothing about capital.

Brown and his team thought a TARP scheme was not for the UK – it was difficult to implement, presenting huge valuation problems, as well as being time-consuming, whereas the crisis was upon them. He thought TARP would involve losses, whereas "If we were to step into the banks in any way I wanted government to be compensated in full, with ownership of a stake, even if it took a long time to be paid back."

However, it showed that the US was now thinking 'systemically.' In New York Brown consulted widely and canvassed opinion, finding that if, as happened, TARP met trouble in Congress, there was scope within the proposal for bank recapitalisation. Some economists including Paul Krugman reinforced his view that there was a need for "massive fiscal stimulus" as well growing support for bank recapitalisation – support which was also expressed by American investors he met. The energetic Brown even managed to summon an impromptu gathering of world leaders to canvas support for what did indeed eventually become a G20 approach to the crisis. With Bush, Brown sowed the seeds for a G20 meeting: "If he supported a meeting I would take responsibility to ensure an agreed policy." Even as Brown was leaving the White House, Darling rang him to talk about the next domino: Bradford and Bingley Building Society had collapsed.

This was the spur for Brown to act on bank capitalisation and, although Brown had high hopes of consensus from the G20 later, Bush, while friendly, and annoyed with Wall Street, had left him with the impression that the UK might initially have to act alone.

The last thing Brown wanted was for the UK to be 'picked off' as vulnerable by the financial markets. He would have to woo the Europeans. However, on the plane back Brown studied the analysis from No. 10, the Treasury and the Bank – Mervyn King was firmly behind recapitalisation now – and told his entourage: "I think we are going to have to do this." He recalls: "I sensed the urgency and the sheer scale of the decision we faced. The only answer to the structural problem was for government to buy into banks."

Although many scoffed at King's long period of resistance, his moral hazard concern was perfectly understandable. Even in 2012, the banks have been behaving appallingly, and the powers that be are only just beginning to get their act together in the face of the one-way bet enjoyed by banks: incentives to take too many risks, while knowing they can be bailed out by the taxpayer. Nevertheless, Brown feared that "we were only days away from a complete banking collapse", with bills not being paid, no money in the ATMs … absolute chaos!

The irony for a prime minister who was an avid socialist in his youth – and most youthful socialists used to salivate about the prospect of "the collapse of the capitalist system" – was that it fell to him to save the system: "The UK economy would face a depression if RBS and HBOS both failed … either we had to step in and accept all the associated risks, or simply leave the free market banking system to collapse."

Although the Treasury had been working on contingency plans for bank recapitalisation, it appeared to Brown that, with its limited resources, the Treasury's experienced staff had been badly run down over the years, meaning Treasury officials had their work cut out on individual banking problems, whereas at No. 10 he and his colleagues could be more strategic. Also, it seems that Brown and King thought Darling was slow to put his full support behind recapitalisation and, notwithstanding various differences before and after they found themselves in the eye of the banking storm, Brown and King seemed to develop a good working relationship during the crisis, and respected each other's intellectual approach.

The people who were really slow to accept the need for recapitalisation were the bankers themselves. Brown, in his book, makes one banker's amazing remark – "All I need is overnight finance" – into a chapter heading.

When Alistair Darling saw CEOs of the banks on the eve of the announcement of bank recapitalisation, he found to his amazement that the heads of the banks diagnosed by the regulators as the weakest denied any need for capital, saying that public acceptance would lower confidence even further. The remark "all I need is overnight finance" was apparently made by the chairman of the Royal Bank of Scotland, a bank about as vulnerable as it was possible to be.

Yet for Brown, "The information I had been looking at was as stark as it was serious: we were facing a situation that risked becoming worse than 1929. No one trusted anyone in the banking system, and people were predicting not a recession but a depression... The financial system was looking over the abyss."

The run-up to the announcement of the plan at dawn on Wednesday, 8 October 2008 was tense and fraught. The markets were almost in free-fall; as Darling says, RBS was within hours of collapse and the cash machines had almost seized up. But still several of the banks were insisting that it was a liquidity problem. There was much bad blood about the origins of a BBC report on Tuesday 7 October suggesting that the banks had requested capital. Quite the reverse. Brown had decided to go ahead, when it was not even clear that the banks would accept. He himself thought it was a gamble: "When I went to bed Sarah was already asleep. So it wasn't until the morning that I warned her that we might have to move out of Downing Street in a matter of hours."

Notes, references and further reading:

1) I have noticed that many people talk as though the financial crisis began with the failure of Lehman Brothers in September 2008. This was certainly dramatic, but it should not be forgotten that, as noted in the text, the rot had set in over a year earlier, in August 2007.

2) The background to Shriti Vadera's interest appears to be that the Treasury wanted to consult bankers on the issue of recapitalisation, but not those who would be directly involved. Shriti Vadera was told by Mervyn Davies of Standard Chartered that the man responsible for managing the bank's liquidity, Macer Gifford, had spotted, from the Bank of England's Financial Stability Report, that UK banks had a serious funding gap – something to which the Bank's 'Financial Stability' experts were certainly drawing attention in the Report, but which the Bank was not, to use a subsequent expression of regret by Sir Mervyn King in 2012, "shouting from the rooftops."

The Treasury had helpful consultations with both UBS and, especially, Standard Chartered. There are those enemies of Brown's who argue that he "stole" the idea. And various people tried to claim credit. The reality was more complicated. The main point is that, after a lot of huffing and puffing, it was Gordon Brown who had the political clout to follow up. One is reminded of one of President Harry S. Truman's great remarks (in the context of the Marshall Plan): "It is amazing what you can accomplish if you do not care who gets the credit."

CHAPTER 11

FROM ZERO TO HERO

"My friend Gordon has the right plan, we must do it in Europe"
(PRESIDENT NICOLAS SARKOZY, OCTOBER 2008)

"Gordon Brown goes from zero to hero"
(TIME MAGAZINE, OCTOBER 2008).

THEN CAME the response of the banks, and the anxious wait for the hoped-for moves by the US and eurozone countries, which would leave the UK looking less isolated and less vulnerable. The initial British announcement had been made on Wednesday 3 October 2008 and – surprise, surprise – RBS suddenly agreed it needed capital, not just overnight finance.

Now, in his finance ministry days Gordon Brown had not been too popular in Continental Europe, arriving at meetings late, and leaving early. But he had cultivated individual leaders, and been on good terms with Sarkozy, when the latter was finance minister. The good relationship continued when Sarkozy became President. In the past, Brown's request to attend eurozone meetings had been embarrassingly rebuffed; but this was a crisis and Sarkozy was a friend. On Sunday 12 October, four days after the UK announcement, Brown was invited by Sarkozy to attend the first meeting of the new euro group of fifteen heads of government. Brown's message to his fellow Europeans was that he believed European banks held some $2 trillion of assets originating from the US, of which a fifth were 'toxic'. Not only were they affected by what they liked to regard as a crisis of Anglo-Saxon capitalism: European banks were more highly leveraged. Brown explained that the problem was capital, and that Europe was up to its neck in the crisis.

"I left the meeting after I spoke and was pleased to learn that there was unanimity on their position. One by one, countries in the euro area and beyond decided to recapitalise their banks, and they would design common European rules for a credit-guarantee scheme like ours." It got better: having raised the subject of bank recapitalisation with New York Fed chairman Geithner and President Bush on his earlier visit to the US, Brown was telephoned by Bush to be told that TARP funds would indeed be used for recapitalisation. On the Monday morning (13 October) the details of the recapitalisation of RBS, Lloyds and HBOS were released. Announcements of bank recapitalisation by Germany and France followed the same day, and the European stock market shot up by 10 per cent – "the biggest ever", Brown pointed out.

The formal announcement from the US came on Tuesday 14 October 2008. Brown noted that at no point in history had governments injected so much money into buying up assets in the banking system, with capital and guarantees running into trillions. Thanks to the extraordinary leadership of a British prime minister who was increasingly unpopular at home, the patient was, in Brown's words, "out of the emergency room and into intensive care."

As recently as at the Labour Party conference a few weeks earlier, Brown's leadership had been under threat, but he had come out with the apposite putdown for both 'the young pretender' David Miliband and the leader of the opposition David Cameron, with "this is no time for a novice." A Labour leader had got on remarkably well with the Republican George W. Bush, and had been taken seriously in an area of finance of which Bush claimed to know little, and it was doubtful at first whether the US Treasury Secretary Hank Paulson was 'getting through' to Bush. One story, which I am assured is not apocryphal, is that Bush at one stage asked: "What is capital?"

Well, capital is the bedrock of capitalism. In his analysis of what had gone wrong Brown was shocked to find that banks had been recklessly using their customers' money, that excessive financial remuneration (and how!) was at the expense of the equity capital banks needed. It was, says Brown, "capitalism without capital." Indeed, "We now know that if British bankers had paid themselves 10 per cent less per year between 2000 and 2007, they would have had more capital, some £50 billion more, to help them withstand the crisis. The extent of the undercapitalisation of our banks was £50 billion, and was exactly the sum put up by the taxpayer for the emergency stabilisation of our banking system."

At least one of the Treasury officials who worked closely with Brown at the time regards the bank recapitalisation moment as Brown's finest hour.

It was certainly a magnificent triumph. Sarkozy introduced Brown to the gathering at the Elysée Palace, with the tribute "My friend Gordon has the right plan, we must do it in Europe." Brown had also acted as an honest broker at times between Sarkozy and German Chancellor Angela Merkel in the interval between Washington meetings and the big day at the Elysée. Merkel was initially against concerted recapitalisation, but was won round by the Brownian offensive.

Sarkozy publicly emphasised that a 'go it alone approach' was not sufficient in the face of the escalating crisis. According to a detailed account in Anthony Seldon and Guy Lodge's 'Brown at 10', eurozone officials subsequently confided to the UK's permanent representative in Brussels that "if they hadn't themselves come up with a package to convince their own markets by the time they opened on Monday 13 October, then their own cash machines might not have opened." Officials were "unanimous in praise of Brown."

A year later, George Parker of the *Financial Times* reported British officials as saying that, although looking back it seemed obvious that a single, one-off rescue was needed, it was not obvious at the time, especially when the US seemed set on a different course. "For a while we were out on a limb", said Brown. And Baroness Vadera, one of the officials most closely involved, confessed to having been "so frightened" at the time.

Given the bizarre delusions of, for example, the bankers at RBS, it was generally considered a masterstroke, in retrospect, to make the granting of extra liquidity conditional on recapitalisation. Parker quoted one Cabinet minister as saying: "It was perhaps Gordon's finest moment ... I'm not sure how many votes there are in it, though." Another suggested that Brown might be more interested in long-term financial reform than in "the nitty-gritty of winning a general election."

But of course he wanted to win that election. And the tragedy for the world may be that, once he had lost he was the last man that David Cameron and George Osborne would nominate for the succession at the IMF to Dominique Strauss-Kahn – who, incidentally, while at the IMF had been a great ally of Brown's on the need for enlightened demand management.

Given his love for so many things American, Brown was particularly pleased with Time magazine's declaration that "Gordon Brown goes from zero to hero" on 27 October 2008. The fact is that, for all the travails of his domestic premiership, Brown was the right leader, in the right place, at the right time for the banking crisis and the subsequent G20 attempt at international policy coordination. Time's Catherine Mayer described him as "pitch-perfect in his Churchillian gravitas, a crisis leader for Britain and the world." And a German commentator compared "moody" Brown with "sociopath" Churchill. Mayer said: "however provocative, the comparison is apt: that just as war allowed Churchill to shine, so does the economic crisis play to Brown's strengths."

One official who worked very closely with Brown throughout this period said: "He knew his stuff inside out. It was his finest hour."

He added: "And you know? After he came out with that Freudian slip in the Commons about 'saving the world' he hated himself for it."

Notes, references and further reading:

1) GB stands for Great Britain and Gordon Brown. It says something for GB's leadership qualities in a crisis that he gained respect from his fellow Europeans despite a long record of doing his best to alienate them. As one long time student of the former Chancellor observed: "His behaviour was often impossible. Even when he condescended to be at meetings, he would look bored, read e mails, read his briefs, bite his finger nails, in fact do anything but look interested."

2) The German commentator was quoted in *Time* magazine, 27 October 2008, in the same article that described Brown as having gone: "from zero to hero".

CHAPTER 12
"SAVING THE WORLD"

"Saving the world" Part two: a $1 trillion dollar rescue plan for
the world's economy (G20 SUMMIT, LONDON, APRIL 2009)

ALTHOUGH the 'saving the world' remark was made after the
rescue of the banking system, it has come to be associated
also with part two of Gordon Brown's remarkable contribution to international economic cooperation, namely the huge
success of the G20 Summit of world leaders in London on 1
and 2 April 2009. This is not surprising, because the preparations for, and conduct of, that summit brought out the best in
Gordon Brown, even if on one occasion there was a memorable
moment when Brown let his guard slip, in front of a President
Obama he had not seen, and the President caught a glimpse of
his hot temper, and how he could tear into his staff. Basically,
however, the event was a triumph, and even the chancellor with
whom he was having so many difficulties conceded: "Gordon
... deserves immense credit for it. If he had not been there, it
wouldn't have happened."

The 'it' was nothing less than an agreement on what Brown
dubbed "a $1 trillion rescue plan for the world's economy", via
a huge boost in the resources of the IMF (principally) and the
World Bank, aimed at stabilising the system after the biggest
decline in GDP, industrial production and world trade since

the Great Depression of 1929-32. Developing nations and eastern European economies had been particularly hit by the collapse of normal trade credit and the general withdrawal of liquidity. Statistics presented to Brown showed a plunge of 20 per cent in world trade during late 2008 and early 2009.

The banking rescue had been one necessary move to avert the collapse of the system, but it was by no means sufficient. In addition to the $1 trillion to restore international liquidity there was agreement on the need to improve the international regulatory structure. Finally, and extremely important, there was a concerted fiscal and monetary stimulus. Brown subsequently noted: "We now know that a total of $3 trillion was injected into the budgets of national economies to take us out of recession."

Well, that was the object: to take us out of recession. But to put it bluntly, as things developed, in practice the G20 summit stopped the rot. The recession continued; but as Robert Zoellick, president of the World Bank observed, the G20 package "broke the fall" of the world economy.

Brown's passionate interest in the alleviation of poverty in developing countries is continually cited by anyone who has worked closely with him, and those eight years as chairman of the IMF's key policy committee, as well as a couple of rounds as chairman of the G7 finance ministers group, had prepared him to take a 'global' view of economics. But there was an additional, more narrowly domestic interest for him in securing international agreement on this scale. With financial market concerns about the British budget deficit, it looked, and was, easier to justify a domestic Keynesian stimulus if others were doing it too.

He has observed with some pride: "In both 1929-30 and 2008-09 global domestic product fell for five successive quarters, the fall amounting to 5 per cent in both periods. In the 1930s, however, the collapse continued for a further eight quarters – two years. In contrast, the collapse of 2008-9 was halted in the three months after the G20 met."

The psychological boost of a well-presented international agreement should not be underestimated. Given what has happened, or not happened, since, it might be going too far to claim that it boosted what Keynes used to refer to as "animal spirits". But at least it seems to have prevented them from being lowered even further.

There was painstaking preparation for the summit. In view of the changes in the world economy, and the growing importance of China and India, Brown recognised that the right forum for such a meeting was no longer the G7. Since as recently as 1991, when the G7 finance ministers met in Bangkok to assess the implications of the fall of the Soviet Union, the G7's share of world output had fallen from 70 per cent to about 40 per cent. China and India had accounted for a tripling of the world's potential workforce in 20 years.

After a preliminary meeting of the G20 in Washington on 15 November 2008, the G20 had emerged as the premier forum for international economic cooperation. But Brown managed to invite a number of other heads of government, so that the meeting in London was more like a G26.

At the November 2008 meeting the G20 had agreed to use fiscal policy to stimulate demand "as appropriate." In the run-up to April, Brown did a lightning tour of major capitals, aiming to win leaders over in advance, and his officials worked overtime. "By the time of the summit I had spoken to every single leader – some several times – to lay the groundwork." He and Obama were keen on fiscal stimulus, but the Germans, who did indeed resort to fiscal stimulus but did not like owning up to it, were difficult over a general commitment. Nevertheless, Brown managed to persuade Chancellor Merkel to sign up to a G20 commitment to boost demand if necessary, which enabled him to claim: "monetary and fiscal action was to be coordinated on a level never seen before."

Brown prepared meticulously right up to the last moment. The evening before, there was a reception at Buckingham

Palace and a dinner at No. 10. He was so determined to get an agreement that he warned them about the lamentable failure of the notorious London Summit in 1933, after which international financial cooperation fell into disarray, leading to protectionism and "all the other terrible events of that decade and the one to follow."

President Obama was so pleased with the way Brown handled the meeting, and with its results, that he described it as "a turning point in our pursuit of global economic recovery." And President Sarkozy, with whom, as noted, Brown developed a good relationship over many years, said the outcome was "beyond what we could have imagined ... all of us are delighted with this result."

Neil Kinnock, who was not there but always kept in close touch with his former protégée from the 1980s and early 1990s, joked that "Gordon's phone bill in preparation for that summit made a significant contribution to the PSBR."

Of the big day, Shriti Vadera, who had worked closely with Brown on 'saving the world', observed: "Gordon told them nobody was to leave the room until they reached agreement. In the old days the sherpas [the leaders' official representatives] drew up the communiqué and showed it to their bosses. This time the procedure was reversed."

Brown observed of his own well-honed technique for chairing meetings, that he owed most to his time spent heading meetings of academics as Rector of Edinburgh University: "I learned that you need to drive meeting towards conclusions and not simply wait for them to emerge."

Notes, references and further reading:

1) The inadvertent "saving the world" remark was made in the House of Commons on December 10th 2008.

2) As a vacuum developed in world economic leadership after the departure of Brown from the scene, enthusiasm for fiscal stimulus gave way to premature austerity programmes, and precious little progress was made in regulatory reform.

Chapter 12: "Saving the world"

Brown believed he had made good progress in securing support from President Obama, Chancellor Merkel and President Sarkozy for an international bank tax to provide a cushion for the future, but this fell foul of the US Congress. His right hand woman for much of the crisis, Shriti Vadera, complained not long ago that the "sense of common cause" among the G20 "has faded with the memory of collective near-death experience" and, as for the bankers, legitimate concerns about the effectiveness of regulatory proposals "masquerade under attempts to return to the old normal of high risks and high rewards." (Where the G20 process went right and wrong, Investing In Change, AFME, 2012).

CHAPTER 13

A GOLDEN MYTH

WHEN CASUAL acquaintances asked me what I was working on and I replied that it was a book about Gordon Brown, a typical response would be "that's a tall order" followed by a pause, then: "Of course he did keep us out of the eurozone – but then again, he sold the gold."

Not only did he 'sell the gold' but he sold it at close to the bottom of the market, and against the strong advice of John Nugée, who was the chief manager of the Bank of England's Reserve management team at the time. For myself, I found that, when I was writing 'The Prudence of Mr Gordon Brown' in 2003-04 there was so little interest in the subject that I did not even refer to the episode. Of course, that was before the price of gold had ascended into the stratosphere.

Keynes had described gold as "a barbarous relic" many years ago, and for decades after the Second World War there was a widespread desire, not shared by the French under General de Gaulle, to downplay the role of gold in the world of international reserve management. Indeed, when the IMF's currency unit – the Special Drawing Right (whose value is based on a basket of leading currencies) was introduced, it was with the specific purpose of producing a 'man-made' asset, reflecting the value of the world's industrial production, and not dependent on the vagaries of gold production and the sweated labour that often went into it.

However, old habits die hard, and gold has an attraction that paper assets do not – especially paper assets that sound rather artificial. Gold from the UK official reserve had been sold before, and, despite the popular impression that 'all' the gold was sold by Brown, in fact the proportion was 55 per cent. But the government went about it in an inept manner, warning the market in advance, at a time when both the IMF and the Swiss National Bank were also planning gold sales. This of course depressed the price of sales, which was at an average of $275 an ounce. By mid-2011 the price had reached $1,800 an ounce.

In Brown's defence there were few experts who ever thought the price would scale such heights, and the value of the 45 per cent of gold stocks that he did not sell obviously did scale those heights. The Treasury itself, unlike the Bank of England, was also keen on selling part of the gold reserves. Indeed, Kenneth Clarke, the previous chancellor, had accepted the Treasury's argument that gold should be sold in return for assets that generate a return, but had been dissuaded by the previous governor Eddie George.

Clarke recalled, when speaking to an audience at the London School of Economics, that Bank officials used to tell him: "Chancellor, if we ever have a third world war it [gold] might be the only means of exchange upon which we could fall back." To which Clarke's reaction was: "If we had a third world war, there would be bigger problems than that." But on that occasion 'Steady Eddie' triumphed.

So Brown did not sell it all, and the Bank's reserves of gold, both those which constitute part of Britain's official reserves and those which it holds for commercial and official clients, remain closely guarded. It was not always thus. A former neighbour of mine was a City of London policeman before the Second World War, and was called in to see the then governor, Montagu Norman, on one occasion as a result of 'an incident'.

It turned out that security in those days had been so lax that an Irish labourer who had been declared redundant on a suburban building site had wandered into the City, entered the Bank's bullion yard, and urinated on the gold reserves. My informant said that, when given this account by the governor, he replied:

"And they talk about 'safe as the Bank of England.'"

Notes, references and further reading:

1) Barbarous relics and Special Drawing Rights: I recall going to a briefing at the American Embassy in London during the late 1960s when the then U.S. Treasury Secretary Henry Fowler waxed lyrically about how SDRs would be backed by real industrial production, as gold became less important for a nation's reserves. Nevertheless, one could not help thinking that, if you were fleeing across a border, a pocket -full of gold might be more useful than a wallet stuffed with SDRs.

2) *Kenneth Clarke and gold*: this episode is covered in Conaghan (op. cit.) and in *The Chancellors' Tales*, Polity, 2006. In answer to questions in a talk at the London School of Economics, Kenneth Clarke said that, while he had always wanted to sell the gold, "I can only say that if I had sold gold I hope I would not have advertised in advance that I was going to ... (and) I hope I wouldn't have been as unlucky as Gordon in judging the time."

CHAPTER 14

RESISTING EURO PRESSURES

IF THERE is one issue over which most people seem prepared to give Gordon Brown the benefit of the doubt it is his opposition, in the face of huge pressure from Tony Blair and many members of the Establishment, to Britain's joining the eurozone. The travails of the weaker members of the eurozone in recent years have most certainly borne out Brown's wisdom in this matter. The Cameron-Osborne team does its best to blame the present problems of the British economy on a combination of Gordon Brown's putative mistakes and the weakness of the eurozone – the European Union being Britain's principal export market. As noted, reports of the culpability of the Brown/Darling chancellorships in the matter of the depression have been much exaggerated. But if there is one charge that one does not hear from the Coalition, it is that Brown kept us out of the eurozone.

This does not, of course, mean that everything is fine and dandy with the British economy. Or that our staying aloof from the eurozone was in any sense some kind of positive influence. What it does mean is that the British government in the last decade at least staved off what would have been a powerful negative force: namely, the loss of flexibility for the exchange rate.

One often hears that 'devaluation is no solution'. There is some truth in this; but only some. When a nation's trading position is unsustainable, because its costs are out of line and it is losing competitiveness, then the exchange rate acts as a safety valve. Downward adjustments are not a panacea, nor are they a sufficient solution to underlying productivity and trading problems. In such instances, devaluation, or 'downward floating' is a necessary, but not sufficient condition for maintaining a reasonable balance between exports and imports, and hence for achieving satisfactory levels of output and employment. In the case of the kind of international recession experienced since 2007-09, the flexibility of the exchange rate is a means of at least alleviating the economic and social pain.

The background to Gordon Brown's admirable and ultimately successful struggle against the considerable pressure on him to join the eurozone is fascinating. The Labour Party has long had an ambiguous attitude towards devaluation of the currency. Labour leaders deeply resent being labelled 'the Party of devaluation' – and, in one instance at least, the label is misapplied, because in 1929-31 the Labour government did not devalue by going off the gold standard. It was the National Government that did this, essentially a Conservative-dominated coalition, although led by former Labour prime minister Ramsay MacDonald. But when the deed occurred, it was in fact a former Labour Cabinet Minister, Sydney Webb, later 1st Baron Passfield, who observed: "Nobody told us we could do that." And it was that devaluation which played a major part in the British economy's subsequent recovery from the Great Depression.

The financial cost and economic attrition caused by the 1939-45 war meant that it was only a matter of time before the pound had to be devalued during the first 1945-50 Attlee government, and the event duly took place in 1949. Again, it was during the Labour governments of Harold Wilson in

1964-70 that another devaluation was eventually forced on a reluctant policy machine in November 1967.

It is by now well established that Gordon Brown, as one of the most influential architects of New Labour, was anxious to bury certain memories of the past. One hang-up was over Labour's association with nationalisation; another was that Labour was the Party of devaluation. A third was Labour's ambiguous, at times openly hostile, attitude to the European Union. The nadir was when in 1983, Labour's electoral platform included planned withdrawal from the European Community.

In 1975 Harold Wilson had called a referendum on British membership of the European Economic Community – which we had only joined as recently as 1973, under the premiership of Edward Heath – largely because of division over Europe within the Labour Party. He contrived a 'renegotiation' of certain of the terms of membership, but the whole exercise was essentially an attempt, which proved successful, to keep the Party together.

Later in the seventies, by which time Harold Wilson had resigned and James Callaghan had taken over, the question arose of whether the UK should join the new European Monetary System (EMS). Callaghan explained in his memoirs: "I favoured the general idea as likely to bring more order into the currency markets of Europe and the world, but quite apart from my technical concerns (the Treasury was rightly raising all sorts of questions, including the wisdom of once again having a fixed exchange rate) I could not travel fast. Many people in the Labour Party remained suspicious of what they thought was too close an entanglement with Europe and this, coupled with my own and the Treasury's belief that sterling was standing too high to make our entry advantageous, led me ... to tell Schmidt and Giscard that we could not enter the European Monetary System at the outset."

In his seminal article 'Britain and the origins of the European Monetary System', the former Cabinet Minister Edmund Dell noted that, in the many protracted Cabinet discussions on the subject, "The PM could always find a reason for postponement." The chancellor, Denis Healey, was agnostic until he realised from a conversation with a senior German official that the hidden agenda from the Germans' point of view was to keep the Deutschmark down, i.e. to restrict the degree to which other European countries could devalue to regain lost competitiveness, given that postwar Germany had traditionally been highly productive and kept its costs down. In order to show goodwill, and in the hope of exerting some influence on European economic policy, Healey and the Treasury came up with the idea of joining the EMS, without participating in its principal component, namely the exchange rate mechanism or ERM. Then, as more recently in discussions about how to help the 'peripheral' economics in the eurozone, the hope was that the Germans could be persuaded to reflate their economy.

Dell records that in a crucial meeting of the key Cabinet committee on the issue, Healey emphasised that domestic political considerations would make entry extremely difficult. It was not clear that the Parliamentary Labour Party or the wider House of Commons would approve entry to the ERM anyway.

Margaret Thatcher, then Leader of the Opposition, seized the opportunity to castigate the Callaghan government over its hesitation about joining the ERM; but she proceeded, during her premiership, to put Labour's performance in the shade with her growing hostility towards the mechanism.

This was one of the few areas of policy on which I found myself agreeing with Mrs Thatcher. But the Establishment and the pro-ERM camp eventually wore her down; the chancellor who finally persuaded her, against her better judgment (or instincts), was John Major, Nigel Lawson having resigned partly over his failure to win her round but principally because of the tension on this issue arising from the presence of Sir Alan Walters advising Thatcher behind the chancellor's back.

Meanwhile, two rising stars of the Labour Party had become strongly in favour of the ERM. John Smith, then shadow chancellor, once told me that part of his motivation in propagating ERM membership and eventual European Monetary Union was simply to embarrass the much more sceptical Tories. But both Smith and Gordon Brown were, I think, also influenced by a more pro-European spirit that is apparent in both Scotland and Wales.

Unlike Bryan Gould, a New Zealander and for a time a star of Neil Kinnock's Labour Party in the early 1980s. Gould, in charge of a Labour economic policy review in the late 1980s, was firmly against Britain's membership of the ERM and any future single currency; he came out with arguments which were just as cogent as those produced more recently about the deflationary bias of the ERM and the proposed EMU. Gould, anti-ERM, was in effect defeated by Brown, pro-ERM, and departed the political scene.

But it was, of course, the Major government that took all the blame of Black Wednesday fiasco of 16 September 1992, when Britain's brief membership of the ERM ended in tears. And when the young *Financial Times* leader writer Ed Balls was interviewed the following month for a job as assistant to shadow chancellor Gordon Brown, one of the first things he had to tell his future master was that he was working on a Fabian pamphlet entitled 'Euro-Monetarism: Why Britain Was Ensnared and How It Should Escape'.

Parts of that pamphlet could have been written by Gould. Yet Balls was going to become Brown's trusted adviser, and to play a major role in shifting Brown's position on EMU.

Ironically, Brown told Balls at the time that he had been supportive of Britain's membership of the ERM because of his fears about Labour's association with devaluation. Yet it was to be the inability to devalue within a single currency zone that was, rightly in this author's opinion, to play a key role in the Blair government's decision, after much shilly-shallying, not to recommend joining the eurozone. (I say 'recommend', because the government was committed to a referendum should it decide in favour.) And it was Gordon Brown, indubitably, who eventually played the key role in taking advantage of the 'opt out' which, to his considerable credit, had been negotiated by John Major at Maastricht in December 1991.

At the time of writing – July 2012 – the very future of the eurozone is at stake and European economies within and outside the eurozone are depressed. The fact that Britain is outside the eurozone does not mean that it is faring noticeably better, or less badly, than countries within. But such are the accumulated problems of the British economy that few analysts doubt that the British economy would be in an even worse state if it had not been for the devaluation of 2007-09 – ironically, a devaluation that took place under the premiership of Gordon Brown, a Labour politician who on his own admission was always haunted by Labour's reputation as 'the Party of devaluation.' But when currencies are 'floating' such adjustments are less traumatic than under 'fixed rate' systems.

Way back in December 1992 Ed Balls had warned in his Fabian pamphlet: "The economic implications of the Maastricht Treaty are dangerous and unworkable ... The mistake is to let economic schemes run ahead of political realities ..." The proposed eurozone required "a much closer degree of social and political cohesion and integration than Europe was likely to achieve ..."

Balls's negative arguments about the eurozone were accompanied by his positive support for making the Bank of England independent. And there was going to be a fascinating interaction between these two policies in the early months of the Blair government of 1997-2001.

As any of his associates will testify, Gordon Brown takes a long time to make up his mind on key issues. He will agonise; he can be very indecisive; and in the case of the policy towards the euro in the governments of 1997-2001 and 2001-05, he made procrastination into an art form. Then there were all the well-documented, political calculations, directed not only against his opponents in the Conservative Party, but also, and not least, against his opponents within his own Party.

In the end he made what is colloquially known as 'the right call' on the eurozone. But it was not without occasional doubts. Indeed, in the run-up to the 1997 election there were moments when various of their colleagues got the impression that it was Blair who was the more sceptical about the euro and Brown the more supportive.

Brown had not finally decided on the independence of the Bank of England until quite late in the day, and, on the timing, very late in the day – indeed, the weekend before the election. Although, as noted, he received great acclaim for the move with the Bank of England, there were a few months of nervousness in the summer of 1997. As one official observed: "For much of 1997 Gordon Brown was more pro-Europe than Tony Blair ... Perhaps the change was due to the success of the MPC, because the real fear was that it was not going to work, that the pound would go through the floor and therefore we would need Europe to support it. I don't know at what point Brown became anti, but I am sure Ed Balls was the influence."

With his own domestic policy initiatives receiving glowing reviews in those early days, and Ed Balls making his views on the euro as plain as a pikestaff, the chancellor's flirtation with the idea of euro membership perceptibly cooled. A famous statement by Brown to the House of Commons on 27 October 1997 effectively ruled out membership for the 1997-2001 term, with even a top Treasury official who was basically in favour conceding that the time was not ripe. This was the occasion when the 'five tests' were officially unveiled – tests not only of the suitability of the pound to join the single currency, but of the sustainability of the single currency itself. Words of Brown's that have an interesting resonance in 2012 refer to whether it would be "a successful single currency."

It was deemed without difficulty that the five tests had certainly not been passed in October 1997, and "making a decision, during this Parliament, to join is not realistic." Another statement of Brown's at the time which sounds prescient, as the present government blames its woes on the eurozone, was: "It is in the British national interest for it to work." Incidentally, it is not without interest that, almost certainly under the influence of Balls, the five tests had been given a public rehearsal the February before the election, when Brown was still shadow chancellor.

The impression that Brown was adopting an ambiguous attitude towards the euro was hardly lessened by his statement in October 1997 that he had left the door open for entry "early in the next Parliament" and had actually told government and business "to prepare intensively" for such a contingency. Some years later, the Leader of the Opposition William Hague asked Blair (7 February 2001, Prime Minister's Questions) whether early meant within two years, to which Blair assented – the "only straight reply" he had ever received from Blair, according to Hague.

Early in the 2001-05 term Brown announced at the annual Mansion House speech (20 June 2001) that the second round of 'tests' would take place. They would be "comprehensive and rigorous". They certainly were. It was a huge exercise, involving intensive work by government economists and outsiders, who took the exercise seriously, even though at least some of those involved suspected that the outcome was determined in advance.

Brown and the Treasury took 'within two years' to mean close to the end of two years. Just over half way through the exercise, in his June 2002 Mansion House speech, Brown declared that this was "perhaps the biggest peacetime economic decision we as a nation have to make ..." High among the considerations was the risk of "repeating past failures of exchange rate management" – i.e. losing the flexibility of an independent pound sterling.

It was not just from Tony Blair that Brown was now being pressurised to be more 'positive' about the euro. Various Cabinet colleagues, including Charles Clarke, were in favour at the time, as were Neil Kinnock, by then vice president of the European Commission, and John Monks, retiring general secretary of the TUC. Wary of these influences, Ed Balls delivered a seminal text on 4 December 2002 (the Cairncross Lecture) which contained so many cautionary notes and references to the disastrous consequences in the past when politics was allowed to triumph over economics, that the inference was obvious. Balls never wavered in his scepticism about the eurozone; Brown may have occasionally, but in the end, after much agonising, he could not see the point in taking the risk.

Blair of course, wanted to go down in history as having taken Britain into the eurozone. Instead he goes down in history for joining George W. Bush in the misconceived venture into Iraq. The respected political commentator Steve Richards even argues that Blair was so keen on the euro, a move which he knew would meet the disapproval of Rupert Murdoch, whom he always assiduously cultivated, that supporting Bush was tortuously connected with joining the eurozone.

The reasoning, according to Richards, was as follows: Blair knew that fighting a referendum campaign on the issue of whether to join the eurozone "would finally place him on the opposite side to Rupert Murdoch's mighty newspapers ... In advance of the intimidating confrontation he wanted to do all he could to neuter the onslaught of his powerful Euro-sceptic opponents."

Richards, who saw a lot of Blair at the time, reports that the prime minister was relaxed about being portrayed as so close to Bush because he feared that his support for the euro might invite a return of accusations that Labour was hostile towards the US. He wanted "to prove unequivocally that his support

91

for Europe did not mean the ending of the so-called 'special relationship'."

Whether this would have cut any ice with Murdoch in the event of the referendum that never took place is an open question. One doubts it. But the very thought that one of the influences on Blair's support for the Iraq invasion was to assist the passage of another potentially disastrous plan, namely British entry to the eurozone, is, if one may resort to the vernacular, mind-boggling.

Another episode which was an indication of the pressure Brown was under to submit on the euro question was the offer Blair made early in 2002, first indirectly via Development Secretary Clare Short, and later directly to Brown to do a deal: support a 'Yes' campaign for the euro in return for the premiership after the deed were done.

For all his overweening ambition and scheming to become prime minister, Brown was not prepared to put his own perceived interest above that of the nation. The longer he had been at the Treasury the more he had been conscious of the weight on his shoulders and the danger of making an historic mistake. The results of the exhaustive economic assessment were duly published on 9 June 2003. They were not 'doctored' and raised many doubts about the idea of joining a flawed eurozone. As noted, in the end Brown saw no point in taking an unnecessary risk, and he has been rightly commended for this.

Notes, references and further reading:

1) Re Labour and the EMS/ ERM, Dell's account was published in *Contemporary European History*, 1994, One gem - some things never change- was the hope that, by joining the EMS without participating in the ERM Britain would be able to exercise influence on German economic policy. But, as Dell comments, "influencing the Bundesbank is a chimera."

2) I saw a lot of Bryan Gould at the time, and have great respect for him. His account of Brown versus Gould in *Goodbye to All That* is riveting, partly because it was obviously written in haste and tinged with bitterness.

CONCLUSION

ONE OF GORDON BROWN's favourite books – and he is a bibliophile par excellence – is the monumental work by Robert Caro on "The Years of Lyndon Johnson" Like Johnson, Brown devoted much of his career to achieving the highest position in the politics of his nation. Johnson was an extraordinarily difficult man; so, as has been well documented, is Gordon Brown. Johnson was deeply involved in the machinations of politics, and Machiavellian in the sense that Machiavelli himself urged "princes" to be: "Machiavellian" is normally taken to imply cunning and deviousness; but Machiavelli's emphasis was on ruthlessness – the ruthless pursuit of, and exercise of, power.

In Johnson's case, the pursuit appears to have been the pursuit of power for its own sake: he used this power to drive though his lasting achievement, the 'Great Society' programme, which was the issue of the moment. (Alas, there was also Vietnam). From his early years, Brown wanted to help poor and the downtrodden. A public figure who had dealings with him during both the chancellorship and the premiership, and occasionally crossed him, said: "I have this vision of a little Scottish boy looking at the ocean and thinking of what his missionary ancestors did for Africa."

The lesson he drew from the career of his early hero, the Scottish Independent Labour M.P. James Maxton, about whom he wrote a biography, was that it was not enough to be a good, but powerless, socialist. You had to make compromises.

In the early years of his chancellorship he gained a reputation for prudence. But it was always 'prudence with a purpose', just as he had worked his way up the ladder of student politics, the Scottish Labour Party and the Labour Party itself, in the pursuit of 'power with a purpose.'

The irony was that he lost his reputation for prudence in the latter years, and then seemed at a loss and unable to cope when he eventually became prime minister in June 2007. What I hope I have shown in this short book is that, while there were certainly grounds for the accusations of 'imprudence' in the latter years, the degree to which it was 'all Brown's fault' has been much exaggerated; and, whatever was going wrong on the domestic front, he made an enormous contribution to the measures which rescued the world economy in 2008-09, manifesting admirable leadership qualities. He was the right leader, in the right place at the right time, with independent foreign commentators even comparing him to Churchill. It is unfortunate that in his dealings with people he should have alienated the affections and respect of many; but then, anyone who has read War Diaries, 1939-1945, by Field Marshal Lord Alanbrooke, will know how extraordinarily badly behaved Churchill was on many occasions. Alanbrooke complains of "ravings of prima donnas in the shape of politicians" and of "Winston's vindictive nature." When Alanbrooke says: "Never have I admired and despised a man simultaneously to the same extent", he could have been taking the words out of the mouths of Tony Blair, Peter Mandelson, Alastair Campbell and many others who had dealings with Brown.

An official who worked closely with Brown the prime minister says: "The world financial crisis was his finest hour. He was more decisive and had more 'vim' than the other leaders. True, his temper and character were not perfect. But it's funny how we admired the British determination and controlled fury of Churchill and Mr. Thatcher." Others recall how 'Sunny Jim" Callaghan could be quite tetchy in private; how Edward Heath as prime minister (and after) would be chronically 'grumpy', and although she was courteous to her domestic staff, Thatcher could be rude and dismissive of colleagues not least in her attitude towards Sir Geoffrey Howe, her Chancellor and, later, Foreign Secretary.

Brown disarmingly admitted on occasion that he had not realized how difficult the job he had always wanted would turn out to be. "He was best when not battered on all sides," says one official. Also, "he was best when focused on something he believed in. He would know the stuff inside out. When it came to the world financial crisis the other leaders were like rabbits in the headlights. He was the first to move in a decisive way."

Decisiveness, in Brown's case, often came after much agonizing and indecision. We have seen how his thinking, undoubtedly under the influence of Ed Balls, moved in an anti-euro direction. Peter Mandelson, who, given the tempestuous exchanges he occasionally had with Brown, is remarkably fair in his assessment, observed: "He was a passionate, impatient man, who was driven and who drove others around him hard to get things done. But... that did not make him a bully."

The suspicion of Brown's motives with regard to the euro ran deep. For Mandelson, who wanted us to join, "it wasn't that Gordon was necessarily opposed, it was just that there was no way he was going to allow it to happen on Tony's watch."

Now, as a seasoned journalist, I am well aware of the famous watchwords: "Why is this lying bastard lying to me?" Those who saw Brown's evidence to the Leveson Inquiry could hardly believe their ears when the former prime minister seemed shocked at the idea that he or his attack dogs had tried to undermine Blair. Yet when a colleague in the press wrote one week that Brown should relent on the euro in return for the famous 'handover', I happened to bump into the Chancellor and, personally, I was absolutely sure that his rage at the very idea was genuine, as was his anger with my colleague. He wanted Blair's job, but not at the expense of what he considered the national interest.

Of course there were periods of doubt – not about doing such a deal, but about the euro: it was a huge decision, and he took it seriously. He felt a great weight on his (substantial) shoulders.

Thus the Guardian columnist Hugo Young, who was rather obsessed with what he regarded as the importance of Britain joining the Eurozone in order to 'lead' Europe, often raised the issue in so-called 'off the record' meetings with Brown which were later published ['The Hugo Young Papers']. Young maintained that the main feature of Brown's approach to the euro was "his puzzlement – rather than the adamant position he is represented as taking." But this was in October 1997, before the 'British Version' of economic policy – the independent Bank of England with its symmetrical inflation target – had established itself as one of Brown's great "selling points". In the end it had to be the "British national economic interest", not some vague Foreign Office aspiration about leadership. Given the strong tide of Establishment opinion in favour of the euro – just as there had been in 1988-90 for the ERM – Brown compromised by telling business to prepare, while most of the time harbouring serious doubts.

The important, albeit negative, decision not to join the euro evolved during the first and early second term of New Labour's period in office, the definitive news being announced half way through, in June 2003. This, for all the carping and criticism often, it has to be said, brought by Brown upon himself, was an historic moment, welcomed by those of us who did not regard the Eurozone as sufficiently integrated to 'work' as an economic union on the lines of the US, but most certainly bad news for passionate believers in the euro.

As noted, this negative decision was not something to crow about in the sense that it somehow offered a magic solution to Britain's fundamental economic problems. But it did mean that

Britain was able to retain the important economic policy tool of a flexible exchange rate. Given the chronic British balance of payments problem, the loss of the freedom to devalue would be economically damaging – as, for example, Italy has found.

The 'euro issue' was settled under his chancellorship. It was not to be until 2008-09 that Gordon Brown took his place in history as the leader who 'saved the world.' Meanwhile, there was a festering sore: his relationship with Tony Blair and the impact on his behaviour of his deep-seated resentment – "an ambition which consumed him" observed one Cabinet member. Certainly, the waiting and continual strife wore him down. In Greek tragedy, would-be heroic figures are brought down by some fatal flaw. Some people I have spoken to regard Brown's hesitation over calling an election in 2007 as an example of a fatal flaw of indecisiveness and excessive caution, which ruined the rest of his premiership. 'From then on it was all downhill' is a typical observation.

Unlike LBJ, who was Vice President for only a short time before the assassination of JFK thrust him into the job he had always wanted (before the intervention of Lee Harvey Oswald, Johnson apparently used to speculate about the chances that Kennedy's ill health would eventually afford him his opportunity), Brown had waited, and waited and waited. He felt a deep sense of injustice, Tony Blair had weakly promised to step down, changed his mind, and understandably, harboured serious reservations about Brown's character and ability to cope with the job. Mandelson captures this in the following passage:

> Alastair [Campbell] goaded him about why he had been so persistent in trying to drive Tony out of office. 'I did no such thing!' Gordon barked back, his voice showing the anger he felt. 'We had a deal, and he didn't keep to it.'

Mandelson comments: "We didn't know whether to laugh or cry. This was meant to be an opportunity for him publicly to put his anger behind him." The context was a practice session for a television interview with Piers Morgan in the run-up to the 2010 election! The idea was to show the 'human side' of the prime minister. And then, during the campaign itself, came 'the woman from Rochdale.' But back to that 'fatal' decision not to call an election in October 2007. It undoubtedly rocked the domestic side of his premiership. Yet he was there, in place, with all the experience, contacts and knowledge of the financial system that were required for his leadership during the 2008-09 crisis. By now it is obvious that my view is that he will go down in history as having been a more important figure than is generally recognised at present. Moreover, that hesitation and indecision in 2007, from his perspective, is understandable. He waited all that time; something could have gone wrong during the campaign – a 'that woman' incident – and his premiership might have been over within a month. In the end he could not take the risk. When his predecessor James Callaghan did not take the risk in October 1978 he had at least been prime minister since spring 1976.

Brown, like Callaghan before him, had been chancellor before becoming prime minister. In Callaghan's case there was a nine-year gap, including a brief period of Conservative government. Once a chancellor, or finance minister, always a chancellor or finance minister. In West Germany, Helmut Schmidt was very much involved in economic policy when, having been finance minister in the early 1970s, he became Chancellor; in France, Valéry Giscard d'Estaing moved in due course from finance ministry to the Presidency. And it was when those two were in the top position in their respective countries that they hatched the ambitious plan to create the EMS, which led eventually to the single currency.

Much has been made by Brown's critics of his intervention from No. 10 in Treasury matters, not the least of the critics being the man who suffered from that intervention, namely Alistair Darling. If ever a professional friendship was tested, it was between those two, with Darling complaining in 'Back from the Brink' about Brown's attempts to remove him. In mitigation it should be noted, which even Darling concedes, that Brown, when offering him the post in 2007, warned that it would be temporary.

These, as the political commentator Alan Watkins used to say, are deep waters. It seems that Brown really wanted to make Ed Balls his chancellor, but the timing was wrong. Having been Brown's right-hand economist for so long, Balls wanted to be his own man, and run another department, before becoming Chancellor. After much characteristic indecision, Brown offered the job to Darling, and Balls, having been Economic Secretary to the Treasury, became Secretary for Children Schools and Families. Darling appeared to be convinced during his chancellorship that Balls was trying to undermine him; Balls, a keen student of history, maintains that he was conscious of what went wrong when Lawson felt he was being undermined by Sir Alan Walters in 1988-89 – an episode that ended in tears. Balls did not wish to 'do a Walters'.

The main problem seems to have arisen during the brief period, at the height of the Parliamentary expenses scandal, when even Darling's position appeared to be vulnerable, given the arbitrary nature of the way events were unfolding. There was a contingency plan to make Balls chancellor if Darling had to resign, but it all blew over. If Balls had been made chancellor, he would have asked Lord Adonis to be chief secretary.

As one former Treasury man observes: "The relationship between Nos. 10 and 11 is the San Andreas Fault of British government." When things go wrong, it affects the fate of the entire government, as happened all too obviously between prime minister Thatcher and chancellor Lawson. There were serious rows between Brown and Darling, but in the end the government emerged with a balanced recovery plan. With respect to domestic policy, Darling was closer to the Treasury line of aiming at a more rapid decline in the budget deficit than Brown wanted; but even so, as he made abundantly clear after stepping down as chancellor, Darling was also critical of the speed with which his successor George Osborne wished to attack the problem. He insisted that the Conservative plan for the deficit posed a serious threat to recovery, as did Ed Balls, in the notably prescient 'Bloomberg' speech he delivered in August 2010.

There is no doubt that on Gordon Brown's watch New Labour relied too much on the flow of tax receipts from the City. This became a trickle after the onset of the financial crisis. This development, and the recession, had a huge impact on the budget deficit. But when the private sector is depressed, basic Keynesian economics teaches us that the public sector has to fill the gap if the situation is not to deteriorate further.

When Brown's premiership came to an end, the British economy was recovering, albeit slowly. After a 4 per cent drop in real GDP in 2009 – showing the brunt of the impact of the financial crisis – there was a rise of 1.9 per cent in 2010. But this reflected the gentle recovery that was taking place under Brown and Darling, showing the benefit, among other things, of a calculated reduction in VAT and a cautious approach to deficit reduction.

George Osborne, as chancellor, raised VAT prematurely, and knocked confidence severely with his emphasis on austerity and rapid reduction in the deficit. The result, in the words of Ed Balls, by now shadow chancellor, was that the economy "flatlined". At the time of writing GDP was well below its previous peak, yet the worst of the austerity programme had still to come. Meanwhile, the 'cuts' were beginning to affect public services throughout the country. One suspects that, as time goes on, it will be seen that Brown and his colleagues did more for public services such as health, education and the relief of poverty than was recognised at the time.

Notes, references and further reading:

1) cf *The Years of Lyndon Johnson, Vol. IV, The Passage of Power*, Robert Caro, 2012, of which there is an interesting review in the 5 July 2012 London Review of Books.

2) Brown's biography "*Maxton*" was finally published in 1986. He had worked on it for many years.

3) Alan Brooke's *War Diaries* are a great contribution to the history of the war (and Churchill's part in it), during most of which he was Chief of the Imperial General Staff. The writing of Diaries was officially forbidden in the army of which he was head. He got round this by writing them in the form of letters to his wife.....

4) *The Hugo Young Papers*, 2008, were advertised as "Thirty Years of British Politics – OFF THE RECORD", and contain the political journalist Hugo Young's edited notes on decades of private conversations with policymakers and others. But I understand that permission was duly sought for printing what was "off the record" originally, and that few refused, and Gordon Brown was happy to be quoted. Roy Hattersley, by contrast, who was deputy leader under Neil Kinnock, believed that what was 'off the record' should remain off the record.

5) Among works drawn on here are: *The Third Man*, Peter Mandelson, 2011 and, of course, *The Diaries of Alastair Campbell*, who, by definition (of Mandelson) must be the Fourth Man – after Blair, Brown and Mandelson himself.

POSTSCRIPT

WHERE NOW?

If I may briefly introduce a personal note, I should like to emphasise that I myself have known Gordon Brown since the early 1980s, and always found him most congenial and entertaining. Thus I have never witnessed at first hand the "dark side" about which so many people have commented, and which, in the interests of balance, I felt obliged to refer to in this monograph.

Gordon is plainly a prophet more honoured abroad than in his own country, and I think it is very sad that, at least up to the time of writing, a leader who has so much to offer should appear to have gone into retreat.

When I went to see him in his attic office at the House of Commons in late April, I met the Guardian journalist Simon Hoggart just outside the Portcullis House building where I was due to see the former prime minister. When Simon asked where I was going, and I said I was due to see Gordon Brown, he replied "Well, if you are, it will be the first sighting of him this year".

He was only half joking. There have been few public appearances this year in this country, and precious little has been heard from him in Parliament. His occasional bursts into print are more likely to appear in the International Herald Tribune than in the British media.

Most people I have seen in connection with this book complain that our former prime minister has precipitated himself into a long sulk, reminiscent of Ted Heath' s behaviour after he was ousted by Mrs Thatcher when he lost to Harold Wilson in 1974. But at least Heath was prominent on the backbenches, contributing frequently, and with gusto, to the economic debate.

I regard it as tragic that the Britain, which was a founding father of the International Monetary Fund, but has never provided a full time managing director, did not back Brown for the job when Dominique Strauss-Kahn resigned. True, one way or another he had lost allies in the Whitehall establishment. But the main reason, plainly, was the poor state of the relationship between him and the Chancellor George Osborne. By contrast, despite their differences over policy, in the eighties chancellor Nigel Lawson and shadow chancellor John Smith used to get on famously.

In this case, of course, the policy difference also mattered. It suited the Coalition to blame Brown for almost everything, and their strategy of "expansionary fiscal contraction" was, and remains, wholly at odds with Brown's advocacy of a Keynesian approach at both the national and the international level.

I have quoted liberally from the book that Brown published in 2010 but which was largely ignored at the time. It is good that the former prime minister is now involved in UN education work. And there can be little doubt that his interest in developing countries will continue.

But in the manifest absence of impressive leadership on macro economic policy at both the European and world level, it is a tragedy that the man who "saved the world" in 2008-2009 is no longer in the thick of policy.

As it is, as he wrote in "Beyond the Crash", in the manifest absence of world coordination for economic recovery – "something bigger, more imaginative, and more lasting even than the Marshall Plan for Europe: a constantly updated plan for economic growth" – the conclusion is terrifyingly clear: "we now face ten years of low growth in Europe and America. It will be a lost decade of mass unemployment in the developed world and mass poverty in the developing world".

INDEX

AIG 61
Adonis, Lord 99
Balls, Ed 40, 42, 44, 87, 88–91,
  95, 99, 100
Bank for International
  Settlements 15
Bank of England xiv, 1, 4, 5, 11,
  12, 14, 15, 24, 25, 27, 28, 34,
  36-38, 42, 49, 52, 56, 61, 79-81,
  88, 89, 96
Barro, Robert
Barroso, Jose Manuel 50
Bank of Credit and Commerce
  International 15, 28
Bear Stearns 37, 39, 51, 52
Berlusconi, Silvio 50
Bernanke, Ben 57
Black Wednesday 23, 43, 44, 87
Blair, Tony xiii-xv, 2, 3, 5, 11, 18,
  23, 24, 33, 36, 39, 40, 45, 46,
  56, 83, 87-92, 94-97, 101
Blank, Sir Victor 61
BNP Paribas 37, 39
Bradford and Bingley Building
  Society 63
Bretton Woods System 34
Brown, Gordon
  and Asian Financial Crisis 34

achievements of xiv, xv, 59, 92
apparent disorganisation
  of 58
boom and bust 4, 5, 6, 17, 23,
  35
brief honeymoon period as
  Prime Minister 45
'Brown Boom' versus
  'Lawson Boom' 7, 24,
and financial regulation
  27-28, 34, 38, 42
and IMF 29
intellectual influences of 57,
  93
love of America, 70
"prudence" of 2, 3, 7, 94
as Rector of Edinburgh
  University 76
role in 2005 election 5
and social justice 2, 73, 100
Professional and working
  relationships with
  Alan Greenspan, 14, 34
  Alastair Campbell, 97
  Alistair Darling, 12, 58,
    98, 99
  Angela Merkel 75, 77
  Barack Obama 76

Conservative opponents 35, 70, 83
Ed Balls 88, 99, 100
Eddie George 5
George W. Bush 68-69
Mervyn King 52
Nikolas Sarkozy 67, 77
Peter Mandelson, 95, 97
Tony Blair xv, 3, 8, 11, 46, 92, 97
unfair criticism of, xi, 24
temperament and alleged character flaws xiv, 46-47, 71, 88-89, 93, 94, 95
youthful aspirations of, 39, 51, 62, 64
Brummer, Alex 21, 44
Budget deficits
Bush, George W. 50, 55, 59, 62, 63, 68, 69, 91
Bush administration 59
Cameron, David 8, 35, 45, 46, 68, 70, 83
Campbell, Alastair 94, 97, 101
Caro, Robert 93, 101
China 7, 75
Clarke, Charles 91
Clarke, Eoin Dr 18
Clarke, Ken
Clause 4
Callaghan, James 31, 32, 43, 46, 85, 86, 94, 98
Clinton, Bill 13
Crosby, Sir James 51
Darling, Alistair 11, 12, 36-38, 40, 41, 44, 46, 49, 51-53, 58, 61-65, 83, 98-100
Davies, Sir Howard 21, 38, 41

d'Estaing Giscard 32, 33, 43, 85, 98
European Central Bank (ECB) 14, 37
Fannie Mae 56, 61
Financial Services Authority 15
Freddie Mac 56, 61
G7 11, 17, 36, 50, 52, 57, 74, 75
G20 33, 47, 59, 63, 70, 73-75, 77
Galbraith, JK 14
Geithner, Timothy 68
George, Eddie 1, 5, 6, 80
Gold 79-81, 84
Gould, Bryan 87, 92
Government debt 5
Great Crash, 1929 13
Greenspan, Alan 12-14, 34, 35
Hague, William 90
Harvard University 34
HBOS 51, 55, 61, 62, 64, 68
Healey, Denis 3, 31, 32, 43, 86
Heath, Edward 3, 85, 94, 103
Howe, Sir Geoffrey 95
International Monetary Fund 11, 29, 104
Iraq 5, 9, 23, 24, 45, 91, 92
Johnson, Lyndon Baynes 93, 97, 101
Johnson Matthey Bankers 15, 28
JP Morgan Chase 51
Keynes, J M 8, 31, 43, 59, 74, 79, 104
King, Mervyn 1, 6, 16, 23, 28, 34, 38, 40, 44, 54, 63
Kinnock, Neil 76, 87
Kirkcaldy 14
Krugman, Paul 63
Labour Party xiv, 31, 32, 39, 40, 43, 45, 68, 84-87, 94

Index

Lawson, Nigel 17, 20, 24, 39, 86,
99, 104
Lehman Brothers 61, 65
Lloyd George, David 1, 11
Macleod, Iain 3
Macmillan, Harold 18, 19
Major, John 2, 8, 18, 86, 87, 88
Mandelson, Peter xiii, 2, 94, 95,
97, 101
McCarthy, Callum 38, 41
Merkel, Angela 50, 69, 75, 77
Monetary Policy Committee
4, 56
Moral hazard 34, 40 42, 52, 53,
63
Murdoch, Rupert 91, 92
Nixon, Richard 32
Northern Rock 36-42, 45, 49,
51, 53
Obama, Barack 73, 75-77
Osborne, George 8, 35, 46, 59,
70, 83, 100, 104
Paulson, Hank 69
Peston, Robert 38, 41
Pohl, Karl-Otto 21
Prodi, Romano 50
quantitative casing (QE) 57
Rajan, Raghuram G. 12-14, 16, 21
Rawnsley, Andrew 3
Richards, Steve 46, 48, 91
Royal Bank of Scotland 51, 55,
64
Salisbury, Lord 3
Sarkozy, Nicolas 50, 51, 67, 69,
76, 77
Schmidt, Helmut 32, 33, 43, 85,
98
Smith, Adam 14, 33
Social housing 18–20

Special Drawing Rights 81
Strauss-Kahn, Dominique 47,
70, 104
Summers, Larry 13
Tax credits 2
TARP 16, 63, 68
TUC 91
Thatcher, Margaret 2, 4, 18, 51,
71, 86, 94, 95, 99, 103
Treasury 1, 2, 6-9, 11, 13-15, 29,
36, 40, 42, 43, 46, 51, 52, 58,
61, 63, 64, 69, 80, 81, 85, 86,
89, 90, 92, 98, 99
UK xv, 18, 21, 24, 31, 36, 47, 50,
53, 56-58, 61-64, 67, 69, 80, 85
UK economy
- debt to GDP ratio 9
- inflation 11-14, 16, 23, 24, 36,
41, 96
- regulation 5, 13, 15, 27, 28,
34, 35, 41, 42, 49
- unemployment 24, 104
unfair criticism of, xi, 24
Vadera, Shriti 57, 58, 70, 76, 77
Vansittart, Nicholas xiii, 1, 30
Volcker, Paul 39
Walpole, Robert xiii
Walters, Sir Alan 86, 99
White, William 15
Wilson, Harold 39, 84, 85, 103
Winter of discontent 47
World Bank 33, 73, 74
World Economic Forum
(Davos) 49
Zoellick, Robert 74

109